BUILDING REASONING AND PROBLEM-SOLVING SKILLS

IN CHILDREN WITH AUTISM SPECTRUM DISORDER

T0385408

of related interest

The ASD Feel Better Book
A Visual Guide to Help Brain and Body for Children on the Autism Spectrum
Joel Shaul
ISBN 978 1 78592 762 1
eISBN 978 1 78450 627 8

Autism and Everyday Executive Function
A Strengths-Based Approach for Improving Attention,
Memory, Organization and Flexibility
Paula Moraine
ISBN 978 1 84905 725 7
eISBN 978 1 78450 089 4

A Practical Guide to Happiness in Children
and Teens on the Autism Spectrum
A Positive Psychology Approach
Victoria Honeybourne
ISBN 978 1 78592 347 0
eISBN 978 1 78450 681 0

Understanding Sensory Processing Disorders in Children
A Guide for Parents and Professionals
Matt Mielnick
ISBN 978 1 78592 752 2
eISBN 978 1 78450 568 4

BUILDING REASONING AND PROBLEM-SOLVING SKILLS
IN CHILDREN WITH AUTISM SPECTRUM DISORDER
A STEP BY STEP GUIDE TO THE THINKING IN SPEECH® INTERVENTION

JANICE NATHAN, MS, CCC-SLP
AND BARRY R. NATHAN, PHD

Jessica Kingsley *Publishers*
London and Philadelphia

Figure 2.1 used with permission of George Boeree.
Table 3.2 is reproduced from The Source: Development of Executive
Functions, Second Edition (p.11), by Jill K. Fahy and Gail J. Richard,
2017, Austin, TX: PRO-ED. Copyright 2017 by PRO-ED, Inc.
Reprinted with permission. No further duplication allowed.
Figure 6.1 reprinted from New Ideas in Psychology, 22, Charles Fernyhough, Alien
voices and inner dialogue: towards a developmental account of auditory verbal
hallucinations, Pages 49–68, Copyright 2004, with permission from Elsevier.

First published in 2018
by Jessica Kingsley Publishers
73 Collier Street
London N1 9BE, UK
and
400 Market Street, Suite 400
Philadelphia, PA 19106, USA

www.jkp.com

Copyright © Janice Nathan MS, CCC-SLP and Barry R. Nathan, PhD 2018

Front cover image source: iStockphoto®. The cover image is for
illustrative purposes only, and any person featuring is a model.

Library of Congress Cataloging in Publication Data
A CIP catalog record for this book is available from the Library of Congress

British Library Cataloguing in Publication Data
A CIP catalogue record for this book is available from the British Library

ISBN 978 1 84905 991 6
eISBN 978 1 78450 390 1

Printed and bound in Great Britain

*This book is dedicated to
our brother and brother-in-law, Samuel Bushnick, whose
generosity is boundless and who inspires us every day.*

Contents

PART IV: LITERACY DEVELOPMENT

PART V: FINAL THOUGHTS

Preface

Growing Up in a Family with Autism[1]

Nine years ago—at the age of 50—my brother received a diagnosis of high-functioning autism (HFA). Up until his diagnosis, he had grown up with the label "learning disability." When Sam was diagnosed with HFA, I went through what I call a mini-mourning period. I had mixed feelings of shock, disbelief and sadness. My brother was no longer someone with a learning disability, but someone with autism! I now realize that my mother was also on the autism spectrum (but that is another story for another time).

As a result, I have spent the last two years revisiting my entire childhood, because the childhood I thought I had, had disappeared and was replaced by a mom and a brother who were on the spectrum. I now recognize that there are three cousins on my mom's side who are also very quirky and different, and if not actually on the spectrum, have some of the characteristics of someone on the spectrum. Resolving this disconnect has helped me so much in my relationship with my brother. I have always admired my brother for his quiet dignity and perseverance through the enormous challenges he has faced in his lifetime. He is intellectually my superior, and one of the most generous and thoughtful people I know. His diagnosis of HFA has allowed me to become much more accepting of his unique perspective on life.

---

1   Adapted from "Growing up in a family with autism" (Nathan, 2011).

And yet, I can still become uncomfortable sometimes when he says or does something that might be construed by others as sarcastic or lacking in empathy.

Growing up, my brother had severe speech, language and communication delays. He was nonverbal for the first few years of his life, and would wander off in stores. Whenever we went shopping, my mother would put a "child leash" on my brother as he was very inconsistent in attending to his name. In fact we called him "Sammy boy," because my mom told me that this tended to help my brother "hear" his name. When Sam did begin speaking, my parents and I were the only ones who understood him. I was his translator until he was nine. Even after that, unfamiliar adults had trouble understanding Sam much of the time. It's hard for me to know what Sam "sounded" like when he talked, because I understood everything he said, even when others couldn't. When I look back, I realize that we didn't engage in true back-and-forth conversation. We played games together that I initiated, or I would tell him stories and he passively sat and listened.

Academic learning was an absolute nightmare for my brother. His frustration and anger grew as he watched everyone else around him learn to read and socially interact so easily and effortlessly. After he was given his label of learning disability, he was placed in the one-size-fits-all special education room that existed back then. There he stayed until high school when he transferred to a vocational-technical high school and trained to become a machinist.

In retrospect, I believe not having the label of autism as a child may actually have benefited Sam, in that my dad had the same expectations for him as he did for me. We were both expected to clean our rooms, get up for school and do homework. The routine of homework for me was that I would go in my bedroom and close the door. Sam's homework routine was very different. Every evening my dad would say, "Sam, it's time to read." Sam would begin to yell, "No, I don't want to." My dad would then have to drag my screaming and kicking brother to their reading spot, and Sam would have to read a Dr. Seuss-type book over and over again. I agree with the writer and researcher Temple Grandin that expectations should be placed on all children. We need to assume that all children can learn, and *then* see what they can do by themselves and what they need help with. My brother is a living example of this philosophy. Sam was a non-reader until middle school. My dad saw his son as a child who was capable of learning, but needed support to achieve academic success. My brother is now an avid reader who loves to read science fiction books.

I am fortunate in that as Sam got older, his ability to communicate with language improved. Now as an adult, he is employed full time, drives and has a social network through the Advisory Board on Autism and Related Disorders (ABOARD). It is interesting how our life experiences impact our career choices. I now know that growing up watching my brother struggle to succeed academically and socially shaped my decision to become a speech–language pathologist. I never thought about it at the time: when I looked over the curriculum for "communication sciences and disorders," I felt like I had come home! In graduate school, I had no idea that I would end up specializing in providing language intervention for children with autism spectrum disorders (ASD). It just sort of happened late in my career, after I moved to Pittsburgh from Arizona in 2001. I took a job at The Children's Institute, and for the first time was seeing a significant number of children on the spectrum. That's when everything "clicked" and I realized that this is what I was meant to be doing!

As an adult and a speech–language pathologist, I am very empathetic with the families who have children or siblings on the spectrum. I am passionate and dedicated to helping children like my brother have easier days than he did, and empower them to believe in themselves. I don't believe that I would understand children with ASD the way that I do if I had not grown up with my brother and my mom.

I've always believed that things happen for a reason. My brother (and my mom) have given me the unbelievable gifts of compassion, tolerance, and having the luxury of being able to step out of the "box" that all of us neurotypicals live in, and to appreciate and enjoy the different world that "out of the box" thinkers like my brother live in every day of their lives.

Note: To aid readability and to avoid favoring either gender, I have alternated between male and female gender pronouns in each chapter.

Part I

BEING ON THE AUTISM SPECTRUM

When young children get angry, they sometimes hit or bite or kick. That doesn't mean they're "bad." That's just how they show they're mad. They don't yet have words to tell us how they feel.

Fred Rogers of children's television program,
Mister Rogers' Neighborhood

CHAPTER 1

Understanding Autism Spectrum Disorders

What it's Like to Live on the Autism Spectrum

Imagine if in every situation in your day-to-day life, good or bad, happy or sad, you had difficulty expressing your thoughts or feelings. Imagine what your life would be like in a classroom if your brain had difficulty retrieving the words it needed to think—to reflect on what was said, to compare or contrast it to what you already knew, to reach a conclusion or opinion, even before you were ready to express yourself verbally. Imagine your feelings as these situations built up, over and over again, in a classroom situation or in a new situation. Wouldn't you get frustrated? Wouldn't you, out of frustration, want to hit something (or someone—even someone you love and respect)? Might you want to throw something, or bang your head against the wall? This is what they experience...every day. Expressing our thoughts and feelings requires language.

We think in speech. The most important theme of this book is that the disruptive and dysfunctional behaviors we observe in children with ASD *are not intentional*; instead they result from the child's language deficiencies. *No child wakes up determined to have a bad day.* Their inability to use language for reasoning and problem-solving, even for what seems to us simple problems, is frustrating. And as frustrating as it may be for us as parents, teachers, friends or therapists, it is even more frustrating for the child!

Children with ASD become easily and quickly overwhelmed when we require their brains to do that which is most difficult for them: using language for reasoning and problem-solving. Without the ability to use language for reasoning and problem-solving, that is, to *think in speech*, children with ASD become frustrated. Without the ability to use language to help themselves organize their thoughts to stay calm, they become dysregulated; they may repeat themselves or scream or throw something. These behaviors reflect their frustration; without being able to think in speech, their brains cannot help them answer a question or cope with the situation.

Now, recall all the times you have heard someone in the face of these dysregulatory behaviors, rather than show empathy, make a comment similar to one of the following:

"Johnny can be so manipulative."

"Suzie knows what to do; she's just choosing not to do it."

"Billy is often noncompliant."

Is this fair to the child with ASD? Empathetic adults would never lecture a child who was blind for walking into them; they would not chastise a child in leg braces for not "keeping up"; and they would not make fun of child with multiple sclerosis for trouble with coordination.

A Day in the Life—Our Mind Is Always Making Predictions

Everyone, from the moment we wake up to the moment we lie down to go to sleep, makes predictions about what will happen next. We do this mindlessly, without thinking about doing it. When we leave one room and enter another, we make predictions about what will happen, or won't. We make these predictions based on our past experiences of entering this room before, or entering different rooms in the same house, or entering rooms like this one but in other homes. The ability to predict our next moment allows us to calmly enter a room we've never been in. Our brains make these predictions virtually automatically, often referred to as mindlessly, that is, without consciously thinking about it.

Similarly, when I go into a grocery store, I know what to expect because I've been to grocery stores before. I know where the shopping carts are, I know which way to go as soon as I enter the store. Even when I go into a new grocery store for the first time, I assume that the first things I will see are fresh fruits and vegetables because that's what I've experienced when entering most other grocery stores. In fact, if it's not the first thing I see, I feel disoriented. And it's not until I see the fresh produce section that I relax and go about the rest of my grocery shopping, almost mindlessly.

Children with autism do not make these predictions. Their brains do not automatically retrieve examples of past experiences of going into a grocery store, and even if they did, their brains do not automatically compare and contrast this experience with past experiences. Instead, going to the grocery store is a new experience—again. This is why they can become suddenly and severely dysregulated entering a place that they have been to many, many times in the past.

The same is true with meeting people. When my spouse and I enter the home of a new friend, we automatically make predictions about what will happen, and what won't. We make these predictions based on our past experience of visiting new friends. If this is a friend of my spouse, it takes me longer to relax; my spouse has met this person in other situations before, but I haven't. At first I am comparing and contrasting this new friend with past friends to know what to say and what not to say. But as this new experience unfolds in a manner similar to when I've met other people, I relax, and I am able to enjoy the rest of the evening mindlessly.

These are typical examples from a neurotypical person's day. But this is not what most individuals on the autism spectrum experience. For many individuals with autism, the cognitive processes needed to compare and contrast a new experience with a prior one do not happen automatically, and only happen after many, many experiences in the same situation or with the same person. Because individuals with autism are not making moment-to-moment, second-to-second predictions about what will happen next based on their prior experiences, they experience what psychologists call *anticipatory anxiety*. Anticipatory anxiety is the apprehension of an event before it happens.[1] The apprehension is due to anticipating a negative event. The "meltdown" often experienced by individuals with autism—

---

1   Definition from the online Psychology Dictionary (www.psychologydictionary.org). The research related to anticipatory anxiety is discussed in Chapter 4.

screaming, crying, biting, hitting, and so on—is the result of their inability to calmly predict what is likely to happen based on similar situations in the past. In effect, they are experiencing a panic attack due to fear of the unknown.

Right Diagnosis/Wrong Diagnosis

Imagine a doctor taking vital signs of an individual, finding the individual's heart rate, pulse and rate of breathing were all elevated. A reasonable conclusion might be that the person is having or is about to have a heart attack; the best course of action would be to get this person to a hospital as quickly as possible. But what if, unknown to the doctor, this same individual had just run a race? In this case, the diagnosis would be completely wrong. The doctor would know that the symptoms were the result of the physical stress caused by having just run a race. And likewise, the recommended action, sending the person to the hospital, would also be wrong.

Likewise, upon seeing a child with autism having a meltdown, too often adults assess the child's behavior and reach the wrong conclusion. The wrong diagnosis is that the child is seeking attention; the right diagnosis is that the child is experiencing stress. If we believe the child is seeking attention, the adult is likely to take action to extinguish the behavior, either through withholding reinforcements, such as ignoring the child, or through punishment, telling the child to stop: "If you don't stop screaming you won't be able to…" Conversely, if we believe the child is experiencing stress, the adult is likely to comfort the child by explaining what the child is feeling (i.e. he is nervous) and what will happen when school starts: "You're just nervous. You're going to make lots of new friends. You're going to have a wonderful teacher who's going to like you and teach you lots of neat new stuff. You're going to love kindergarten!"

The two different diagnoses by the adult lead to virtually opposite reactions to the child's behavior. The first treats the child as having a behavior problem who is intentionally seeking the attention of the adult. The second treats the child as experiencing emotional stress, and verbally helps the child understand what to anticipate so he can reduce the stress he is feeling. In the first scenario, the adult is trying to solve his *own* problem—"I have a screaming child on my hands."

In the second scenario the adult is helping the child understand the situation so the child can reduce his stress on his own. Understanding this difference is essential to helping the new kindergartener help himself calm down: that is, to develop the ability to self-regulate.

The same is true when children with autism are having a meltdown; we need to look at what *their* brain is experiencing. Their in-the-moment behavior is an indicator of stress. As we will discuss throughout this book, the ability to remain self-regulated is essential for problem-solving, and conversely, the ability to problem-solve is essential for remaining self-regulated.

Thinking in Speech®: A Cognitive-Language Intervention

This book describes a cognitive-language intervention, *Thinking in Speech*, to develop problem-solving skills among individuals with autism spectrum disorders. It is intended to help professionals and families improve the ability of a child with ASD to use language for thinking: planning, pausing and reflecting, that leads to increasing emotional regulation. This approach is research-based, drawing from published studies in cognitive psychology, neuroscience, in speech and language acquisition, and in neuro-imagery. The observable symptoms of ASD reflect a brain with executive functioning glitches. In other words, ASD is a *cognitive* disability, not a behavioral disability. Incomplete or ineffective thinking results in dysfunctional behavior.

Thinking in Speech describes how to help the child develop "inner speech" (Alderson-Day and Fernyhough 2015; Ferneyhough 1996, 2008, 2010). More importantly, using the techniques described in this book will help the child develop his own strategies to recognize and cope with the feelings of stress that accompany independent problem-solving, and avoid becoming emotionally dysregulated. "Inner speech" is the inner dialogue that goes on in our heads during everyday routines. The ability to "think in speech" is critical for flexible behavior and cognition, and is the foundation for effective self-regulation (Vygotsky, 1987 [1934]). Parents use interpersonal dialogues to regulate the child's behavior. Over time, the child internalizes these dialogues, and over time, the child is able to regulate his own behavior by engaging in dialogue with self, in the absence of others (Williams, Bowler and Jarrold, 2012). Interpersonal dialogue becomes intrapersonal dialogue. For example, a child sees cookies on the counter. Mom has told the child that he cannot have a cookie until after dinner. A typical child begins an inner dialogue by silently saying to himself, "I really want a cookie now, how do I go about getting a cookie now without getting in trouble?" As behavioral and neurological research has shown, this kind of linguistic thinking is essential for executive and emotional control, but most children with ASD have not developed this kind of inner dialogue necessary for independent problem-solving (Baldo et al., 2005; Dunbar and Sussman, 1995; Gruber and Goschke, 2004; Williams et al., 2012).

Children with ASD also show a range of problems with executive functioning (Hill, 2004; O'Hearn et al., 2008). These executive functions include planning, cognitive flexibility, response inhibition and working memory (Pennington and Ozonoff, 1996). Individuals with ASD are significantly limited in their ability to efficiently and rapidly formulate, reflect upon, and produce multiple options and instead often remain "stuck" on a single solution. Similarly, their ability to set goals for the efficient planning and performing of future actions is impaired. They also have limited ability to switch course when what they are trying isn't working, which can cause them to appear confrontational or intentionally defiant. Individuals with ASD require specially designed interventions that focus on increasing cognitive flexibility, generating multiple solutions to any given problem throughout their day and applying these skills in their daily routines.

Organization of the Book

Part II, "Autism as a Language and Executive Functioning Disorder," provides an overview of the research foundation underlying the *Thinking in Speech* intervention. Chapter 2, "About the Brain: Neuroscience for Understanding Autism," is a brief overview of neurocognition. At its heart, autism is *not* a behavioral disorder, it is a neurocognitive disorder. When working with children with ASD, parents, teachers and clinicians need to think about what's beneath and behind the observable behaviors to assess what's really going on inside the child's mind. We use this for the child as well, when the clinician explains to the child that she is the child's "brain teacher" and is going to teach the child to "talk to his brain" (Chapter 7). Chapter 3, "Executive

Functioning in Children with ASD," provides an overview of the executive functioning research. The behaviors we observe by children with ASD result from the inability to effectively process information (executive functioning). Chapter 4, "Impulse Control and Emotion Regulation," explains why the cognitive challenges that children with ASD face every day lead to frustration and often result in emotional dysregulation. Chapter 5, "Implicit Learning," is a brief but important chapter. Most of the social engagement rules we know are learned implicitly—that is, almost unconsciously. This often does not happen for children with ASD. Thus they need to be explicitly taught many of the social engagement rules, classroom rules, even dating rules, and so on that neurotypical children have learned implicitly. The final chapter in Part II, Chapter 6, "The *Thinking in Speech* Model of Reasoning and Problem-Solving," puts this all together and presents the comprehensive framework that underlies our intervention. Additionally, we present critical research in inner speech, which is the foundation of how individuals "think," and why helping children with ASD develop inner speech is essential for problem-solving and emotional regulation.

The chapters in Part III, "Developing Inner Speech for Problem-Solving and Social Interactions," describes how we implement the *Thinking in Speech* intervention. In each chapter we've presented detailed dialogues that Janice has with the child during her sessions. In addition we explain why Janice is saying what she's saying, or doing what she is doing. Our intent is to allow you, the reader, to be able to model and adapt these conversations to your own children. Chapter 7, "Setting the Stage for the *Thinking in Speech* Intervention," describes the conversation and activities that Janice uses to develop trust and introduce "talking to your brain." The subsequent four chapters in Part III address how Janice interacts with the child for "Developing Mental State and Emotions Vocabulary" (Chapter 8), "Vocabulary Development for Higher-Level Use of Language for Problem-Solving" (Chapter 9), "Answering Questions Logically" (Chapter 10), and "Mental Flexibility to Generate Multiple Solutions" (Chapter 11). The final two chapters in Part III show how Janice uses dialogue to help the child in social interactions: "Developing Theory of Mind" (Chapter 12) and "Teaching 'Chit-Chat'" (Chapter 13). Embedded in all these chapters is how Janice helps the child to self-regulate, even as she is creating stress for the child, as he struggles with developing these new problem-solving and social skills.

Many children with ASD become frustrated in school, especially beginning in third grade, where education shifts from learning to read to reading to learn. Their teachers, too, can become frustrated when they know that despite their best efforts, they are not able to help the child reach his full potential. They know that what they are doing is not working, but they are not sure what else to do. The chapters in Part IV, "Literacy Development," are techniques that Janice has found to help these children be proficient readers and engaged learners. So many of these children are exceptionally smart, but their neurocognitive and executive function deficiencies get in the way of their ability to show what they can truly achieve academically. As with previous chapters in Part III, we present detailed dialogues that Janice has with the child during her sessions and how she uses her dry erase board, and we explain why Janice is saying what she's saying, and doing what she is doing.

Chapter 14, "Developing Emerging Literacy Skills," describes how she teaches decoding, and separately how she teaches reading comprehension. In addition, she describes how fiction books are an excellent resource for helping the child develop theory of mind; thinking about what was going on in the character's mind requires theory of mind. Chapter 15, "Understanding and Reading Textbooks," describes how Janice helps children learn how to find answers in a textbook. She shows how she helps the child use the structure of a text to understand its content, how to search through a textbook for described content, and how to scan pages in order find the correct answers to questions. These are skills that most children learn implicitly, but that children with ASD need to be taught explicitly. We conclude Part IV with "Note Taking, Teaching Time and Assisting with Arithmetic" (Chapter 16), miscellaneous skills that children use in school, at home, and to help them stay organized.

We conclude in Part V, "Final Thoughts," with our last chapter, "Reminders When Implementing *Thinking in Speech*" (Chapter 17). We go over several DOs and DON'Ts when working with a child with autism, which can cause a lack of self-confidence and dysregulation.

Part II

AUTISM AS A LANGUAGE AND EXECUTIVE FUNCTIONING DISORDER

Between stimulus and response there is a space. In that space is our power to choose our response. In our response lies our growth and our freedom.

Author unknown; attributed to Victor E. Frankl

CHAPTER 2

About the Brain

Neuroscience for Understanding Autism

The brain is an incredible and incredibly complex organ. At all times, our brains are constantly controlling our basic functions. Breathing, digesting food, maintaining our heartbeat so that blood flows throughout the body, sensing the world around us visually (sight), aurally (sound), tactically (touch), and through taste and smell, as well as providing for its own maintenance and the ongoing maintenance of every organ, tissue and cell within the body. All of this happens automatically, that is, without higher-order thought. This is referred to as the autonomous nervous system.

Our brains also control our thoughts, our actions and our emotions. On a constant basis, our brains are integrating sensations and information from outside the body as well as inside the body. Moreover, our brains must make sense of this information—in the moment, and in memory. Our brains must manage information across time, differentiating and combining thoughts, actions or emotions that happened in the past with thoughts, actions or emotions that are happening in the present. It provides us with the ability to both sense fear and interpret fear and, in response, stimulate biological resources needed to act when faced with a fear-provoking situation (e.g. providing more oxygen and more blood to certain biological systems) while turning off other systems that might interfere with action (e.g. digestion). For the most part, it does all of this unconsciously.

At the same time, the brain allows us to reason and problem-solve, to consciously think about things. Some of these thoughts lead to actions. In some cases, the brain acts on its own to activate muscles in the body to move (pulling your hand away from a hot surface, or jumping at a sudden noise). In other cases, the action is intentional, to proactively scan in search of a visual objective, or to move in the direction of a person we want to engage. In the latter cases, the brain must activate the psychomotor system. It must combine thoughts with muscles and engage in both gross body movement (move a limb, turn the head) and fine motor control (picking up a pencil, focusing on a specific visual target).

Visually the brain must distinguish things in the distance from things up close, differentiate colors and shapes, and relate them to objects. Auditorily the brain must differentiate irrelevant noise from specific sounds. This includes not only the infamous cocktail party phenomenon, where a person can hear her name spoken from across a room, but also being able to engage in conversations in a noisy environment. Tactilely, it must differentiate soft objects from hard objects, or cold from hot, while at the same time sending signals to the limb to grip harder or let go, or to ignore stimulation in some areas while focusing on others (e.g. to ignore how the chair feels while sitting, and focus on the person with whom you are speaking). Kinesthetically, it must sense where one's body or the limb of the body is in space and time, and how to move it to where the person wants it to be. That the brain does all of this mindlessly (without conscious thought), repeatedly and correctly is incredible.

Unfortunately in individuals with autism, some of the brain's ability to integrate sensation, thoughts and action is imperfect. Having an appreciation for the neuroscience of autism is not merely important for understanding autism research. As a therapist, "owning" the idea that autism is a neurological disorder helps keep my focus on finding ways to better understand how what I do and say may be interpreted by the child's brain.

Neurons and Neurotransmitters Made Simple

The brain contains over 100 *billion* neurons (nerve cells). Each neuron receives signals from one to a hundred thousand other neurons, and in turn transmits signals to one to thousands of other neurons. Transmissions take place both electrically, within each neuron, and chemically, in the process that transmits signals across the gaps between neurons. Neurons can be very short, connecting other neurons within the same part (lobe) of the brain; very long, starting in the brain, then passing through the brain stem and connecting to other parts of the body; or somewhere in the middle, connecting one part of the brain to other parts of the brain.

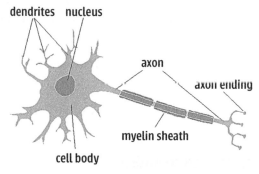

Figure 2.1 Neuron
Image by George Boeree. Used with permission.

Figure 2.1 is a picture of a single neuron. Transmission within a neuron is electrical; transmission between neurons is chemical, via neurotransmitters. Neurons transmit signals in only one direction, from dendrites to the axon; they cannot go in the other direction. Neurotransmitters, chemicals and proteins from preceding neurons are picked up by the dendrites, transmitted through the cell to the axon, and out the axon endings (the synaptic buttons) to the subsequent cells. Neurotransmitters are released from the synaptic buttons at the end of the axon, travel across a gap, the synapse, where they are picked up by the dendrites of the next cell(s). Both dendrites and axon endings have multiple, and in some cases multiples of multiple, branches. (Think of the branches of trees or a tree's root structure.) As noted, each cell takes in signals (via the neurotransmitters) from one to thousands of cells, and subsequently passes on signals to thousands of other cells. Some of those other cells, both the receiving and the transmitting cells, may be located within the same brain lobe, or in other brain lobes, or in other parts of the body. Learning and development are both the cause and the result of more and differentiated branches at both ends of the nerve cell.

A thorough description of the role of neurotransmitters is beyond the scope of this book. What we have come to appreciate is that neurotransmitter systems add to the complexity of how the brain functions. Each neurotransmitter system is affected by:

- where in the brain the system is located, including where the cell bodies of the neurons are found and where the axons extend to

- how many different types of receptors each neurotransmitter binds to, and whether these receptors affect ion flow or protein flow

- the behavioral effects of the neurotransmitter systems, and their interaction.

(Adapted from Pliszka, 2003)

Neuroscience Applied to Autism

Dinstein et al. (2012) describe autism as a developmental disorder characterized by three "core" behavioral symptoms (social difficulties, communication problems, and repetitive behaviors) (American Psychiatric Association, 2000), and a long list of "secondary" symptoms (e.g. epilepsy, intellectual disability, motor clumsiness and sensory sensitivities). Some autism research has focused on specific areas of the brain that exhibit abnormal functional responses in social/ cognitive tasks (Chiu et al., 2008; Dapretto et al., 2006; Humphreys et al., 2008; Pelphrey et al., 2005; Redcay and Courchesne, 2008— all cited in Dinstein et al., 2012), leading to assumptions that autism is associated with dysfunctions in specific areas of the brain (Dinstein et al., 2012). However, a growing consensus is emerging that autism is a *general* disorder of neural processing (Belmonte et al., 2004; Dinstein et al., 2012; Minshew, Goldstein and Siegel, 1997) which affects multiple brain systems.

Dr. Jay Giedd, a neuroscientist at the National Institute of Mental Health, uses language as an analogy to describe brain activity:

Different parts of the brain act like letters of the alphabet...by the time a child is eight months old, the letters are there—the basic connections have formed in the hippocampus or the prefrontal cortex, say—but then through experience, those neural letters activate in patterns to form words, sentences and paragraphs of thought. (Reported in Sparks, 2012)

For individuals with autism, these connections among different parts of the brain are inefficient or ineffective. Researchers refer to this as "underconnectivity" (Just and Keller, 2013; Just et al., 2007; Just et al., 2013). "[U]nderconnectivity compromises the brain's ability to communicate information between the frontal cortex—the brain area involved in higher order social, language and executive processes, and abstract thought—and other areas [of the brain]" (Just and Keller, 2013, p.2).

The Neural Basis of Social Interactions

Our brains are designed to cognitively process the behaviors of others (Spunt, 2013). Researchers have found that the same group of neurons fire when we *perform* an action as when we *observe* the same action in someone else (Rajmohan and Mohandas, 2007). Researchers refer to this as the *mirror neuron system*, and it involves millions of neurons engaged simultaneously (Spunt, 2013).

Related to, but separate from the neural activity of the mirror neuron system is neural activity associated with individuals' ability to make inferences about other persons' mental states. This is referred to as the mentalizing system. Together, these two neurocognitive systems allow us to understand the actions of others. For example, we observe the motor action of an individual, such as a smile (*mirror neuron system*), and from that we might infer an internal emotional state, such as *happiness* (*mentalizing system*) (Spunt, 2013).

Research in this area is still emerging, but Spunt (2013) suggests that the mirror neuron system and the mentalizing system may at times interfere with each other, or act in a seesaw fashion such that when one system is strongly engaged, the other is strongly disengaged. Listening to others involves active interpretation—that is, mentalizing. We must interpret both verbal utterances (language comprehension) and nonverbal behavior (facial expressions, posture, etc.). This is how we understand not only what the speaker is trying to communicate, but also what the speakers may be hiding, such as the speaker's motives, beliefs, and so on.

This has implications for children with ASD because of their underlying language impairment when listening to another person. As the child disengages her mirror neuron system in order to interpret what is being said: that is, engaging her mentalizing system, she is no longer fully engaging the auditory system, which is processing what the speaker is saying. The child may miss critical information, but also, critical facial expressions, vocal tones or posture of the speaker, as the child is cognitively engaged in interpretation. In addition, at this time the child may not look engaged, for example not maintain eye contact, which can affect interpersonal rapport (Lakin and Chartrand, 2003). The listener may interpret the child's expression as disinterest, or social disengagement, when in fact the child is working hard at listening— spending additional mental effort to overcome their impaired ability to simultaneously listen and interpret what the speaker is saying.

Neurological Functions, Executive Functioning and Clinical Practice

Table 2.1 shows how both neurological and cognitive aspects on the one hand, and clinical research and practice on the other, address the development of inner speech when a child struggles to answer an open-ended question. When a child struggles to answer an open-ended question, the clinician points out what the child is doing to help the child use words to describe the situation: "When you close your eyes you are showing me you need help. When I hear 'I need help' I can help you. Miss Janice, I need help."

First, the amygdala senses the physiological response (tightening of the gut or other sympathetic nervous system reactions) alerting the child that something is happening, that is, she is in a problem-solving situation. Next, the hippocampus (memory center) retrieves previously learned knowledge, that is, a strategy to solve the problem of what to do when feeling stressed by an open-ended question. Finally, the medial prefrontal cortex generates the response, which is the child independently stating, "Miss Janice, I need help."

In this way, the interpersonal dialogue between the child and the clinician gradually becomes internalized. Over time, the child is able to engage in a dialogue within herself without the aid of the clinician, and is able to regulate her own behavior and become an independent problem-solver.

The clinician models these three steps as a single unit; they flow together. The three steps are used each time the child appears to be unable to respond to the clinician's request (e.g. making a choice, responding to a wh- question, answering open-ended questions). As soon as the clinician observes the beginning of dysregulation, he intervenes with the first step of the process, and continues as needed until the child verbalizes the problem-solving strategy, for example asking for help. This technique is used with every activity: reading books, playing with cards, playing games, and so on. The activity is irrelevant because the clinician is the intervention—helping the child by modeling the development of inner speech.

Table 2.1 Alignment of neurocognitive aspects
with inner speech clinical intervention

Neurocognitive aspects			Inner speech clinical intervention	
Physiological structure	Neurological function	Cognitive interpretation	Problem-solving process	Inner speech prompts (explicit)
Amygdala	"Sensor"	"Something's happening"	Realize it is a problem-solving situation	"When you close your eyes you are showing me you need help."
Hippocampus	"Memory Center"	"Has it happened before?"	Recall a strategy	"When I hear 'I need help' I can help you."
Medial prefrontal cortex	"Decision-maker"	"Take this action"	Decide on and verbalize strategy	"Miss Janice, I need help."

CHAPTER 3

Executive Functioning in Children with ASD

Executive Functions

Executive functions are "the cluster of cognitive skills rooted in the prefrontal structures of the frontal lobe of the brain" (Richard and Fahy, 2005, p.13). Executive functions include a complex combination of thoughts and emotions. Though definitions of executive functioning vary (Salthouse, 2005), in general they include "shifting mental sets, monitoring and regulating performance, updating task demands, goal maintenance, planning, working memory, and cognitive flexibility, among others" (McCabe et al., 2010, p.222). Examples of different descriptions of executive functioning by different researchers are presented in Table 3.1. While there is no universal agreement on a specific definition, most researchers emphasize that the specific components are less important than understanding that the different components act together and simultaneously to regulate and initiate communication, social interactions, self-regulation, problem-solving, learning and memory.

Table 3.1 Descriptions of "executive functions"

| "Executive functioning covers a variety of skills that allow one to organize behavior in a purposeful, coordinated manner, and to reflect on or analyze the success for the strategies employed." | Banich (2004), p.391* |
| "Executive functions are those involved in complex cognition, such as solving novel problems, modifying behavior in light of new information, generating strategies or sequencing complex actions." | Elliott (2003), p.50* |

cont.

"The executive functions consist of those capacities that enable a person to engage successfully in independent, purposeful, self-serving behavior."	Lezak (1995), p.42*
"Executive functions involve the following abilities: 1. Formulating goals with regard for long-term consequences. 2. Generating multiple response alternatives. 3. Choosing and initiating goal-directed behaviors. 4. Self-monitoring the adequacy and correctness of the behavior. 5. Correcting and modifying behaviors when conditions change. 6. Persisting in the face of distraction."	Malloy, Cohen and Jenkins (1998), p.574*
Executive functions involve "shifting mental sets, monitoring and regulating performance, updating task demands, goal maintenance, planning, working memory, and cognitive flexibility, among others."	McCabe et al. (2010), p.222
Executive functions are "those higher-order cognitive capabilities that are called upon in order to formulate new plans of action and to select, schedule, and monitor appropriate sequences of action."	Perry and Hodges (1999), p.389*
Executive functions are "the cluster of cognitive skills rooted in the prefrontal structures of the frontal lobe... They include the ability to anticipate consequences, generate novel solutions, initiate appropriate actions or responses to situations, monitor the ongoing success or failure of one's behavior, and modify performance based on unexpected changes."	Richard and Fahy (2005), p.13
"'Executive functions' broadly encompass a set of cognitive skills that are responsible for planning, initiation, sequencing, and monitoring of complex goal-directed behavior."	Royall, Cordes and Polk (1998), p.378*
Executive functions "refer...to higher-order cognitive capacities, for example judgment, decision-making, planning and social conduct."	Tranel, Anderson and Benton (1994), p.126*
"Executive functioning involves problem solving abilities such as abstraction, planning, strategic thinking, behavioral initiative and termination, and self-monitoring."	Troyer, Graves and Cullum (1994), p.45*
"Executive functions are often referred to as the most complex of human behaviors being primarily concerned with planning and organization of purposeful behavior."	Tuokko and Hadjiistravropoulos (1998), p.143*

* Cited in Salthouse (2005).

Working Memory, Fluid Intelligence and Cognitive Ability

Working memory (WM) refers to the "limited cognitive system involved in the temporary storage and manipulation of information required for task-relevant performance" (Burgess et al., 2011, p.674). It has been referred to as a kind of "cognitive 'engine'…responsible for holding and manipulating temporary solutions, structures, subgoals and sub-products of thinking, before the final result is reached" (Chuderski and Nęcka, 2012, p.1). Silliman and Berninger (2011) describe four executive functions related to attention in working memory:

- *Inhibition* (focusing): understanding what is important from what is not, as in complex math problems or complex written paragraphs, graphs or drawings.

- *Switching* (detecting change and flexibility changing): recognizing that a switch has taken place and that a new focus or interpretation is required, for example a compound sentence in which the focus changed from one person to another, or a math problem in which the measures changed from feet to yards, or from metric to the British system of measurement.

- *Sustaining over time* (staying on task): the ability to remain focused on the task at hand—not mentally "drifting" or becoming distracted by other events in the environment or extraneous thoughts in one's head. (Note: This is to a large extent *not* under volitional control, it is "wired" in the brain.)

- *Self-monitoring* (updating over time): for example, recognizing when one has sufficiently answered a question and that additional information will not improve the answer (e.g. an open-ended response), or realizing one has spent enough time on a question that one can't answer and should go on to the next question.

Individuals with ASD may score lower on traditional tests of general mental ability (e.g. verbal ability, numerical ability, psychomotor ability), because they have less than efficient working memory, not necessarily because they don't know the answer. Likewise, individuals with ASD may have word retrieval deficiencies, or word decoding deficiencies, both of which may adversely affect a verbal ability item, but neither of which is the same as reading comprehension.

Another approach to studying cognitive processing has been the investigation of how, and how well, the brain controls attention to different tasks, generally referred to as dual-processing theories. In this research subjects are given two relatively easy cognitive tasks combined into one more complex activity. For example, subjects are asked to recall words, digits, or spatial orientation, but between these presentations they are required to perform some other attention-demanding computation (e.g. reading sentences, doing simple arithmetic, counting, etc.), which interferes with the memory task. The ability to control attention is a major contributor to individual differences in working memory capacity (Barrett, Tugade and Engle, 2004). Barrett et al. (2004) argue that this research is important not only for understanding the concept of working memory, but more significantly, to understanding how individuals exert control or attention in complex situations: "the ability to keep attention focused on one thing and not let it be captured by other events, be they in the external environment or internally generated thoughts and feelings" (p.554).

Executive Functions and Problem-Solving in Individuals with ASD

Problem-solving has been described as the most complex of all intellectual functions (Goldstein and Levin, 1987). Problem-solving is typically described as a goal-directed cognitive activity that is required in situations with no apparent or immediately available response (Luria, 1966; Sohlberg and Mateer, 2001).

> Real-life problem-solving is distinguished from deductive reasoning tasks by its open-ended nature and, often, the lack of a single superior solution. All the relevant pieces of information are seldom available simultaneously, and the problems can be viewed from a number of perspectives such that solutions involve juggling competing priorities that may differ in importance according to the particular context. Successful solution often involves appreciation of the perspectives of two or more people. (Channon, 2004, p.237)

In its most simplistic terms, problem-solving involves three steps:

1. rapid and efficient ability to retrieve one's world knowledge (based on one's whole life experience—whether one has experienced it, seen it or overheard a conversation not related to him)

2. comparing and contrasting one's world knowledge with any given situation in front of him at any given moment

3. logically adapting one's behavior and/or response accordingly.

Independent problem-solving is difficult for individuals with ASD. ASD is a neurodevelopmental disorder in which atypical cognitive processing development results in language and communication impairments (Klinger, Klinger and Pohlig, 2006). For individuals with ASD, these language impairments can be traced to specific deficits with executive functioning (Hill, 2004). In particular the ability to set goals for the efficient planning and performing of future actions (e.g. remembering to turn in homework, time estimation for going over schoolwork for upcoming tests) is impaired (Brandimonte et.al., 2011). Individuals with ASD have limited ability to switch from plan A to plan B when plan A is no longer working, which can cause a person to appear confrontational or intentionally defiant. Individuals with ASD are significantly limited in their ability to efficiently and rapidly formulate, reflect upon and produce multiple options and, instead, will remain "stuck" on a single solution. These individuals require specially designed interventions that focus on increasing cognitive flexibility, generating multiple solutions to any given problem throughout their day and applying these skills in their daily routines.

The individual's ability to cope in the face of a stressful situation is also a form of problem-solving. Problem-solving in everyday life is *social problem-solving*, where "social" refers to problem-solving that occurs in everyday social environments, such as with parents, teachers, friends, family members, clinicians, and so on (D'Zurilla and Maydeu-Olivares, 1995). Social problem-solving encompasses both intra- and interpersonal problem-solving (Rath, Hennesy, and Diller, 2003). Because children with ASD have impaired language skills, they also have difficulty remaining regulated in stressful situations, of which social situations can be among the most complex. Gaining self-awareness and self-insight into one's strengths and needs, as well as accurately perceiving one's physical state in the moment, requires the ability to think silently in speech.

Problem-solving also involves self-regulation: the individual's ability to cope in the face of a stressful situation. Gaining self-awareness and self-insight into one's strengths and needs, as well as accurately perceiving one's physical state in the moment, requires the ability to think silently in speech. Coping skills are directly related to language and emotional development, which are prerequisites for developing interpersonal relationships, as well as academic and employment success.

Solving real-world problems incorporates both "hot" and "cool" executive functioning processes (Zelazo and Müller, 2002). "Cool" processes are those used in planning, working memory, cognitive flexibility, and so on: traditional problem-solving tasks associated with most neuropsychological measures (Burack et al., 2010). In contrast, "hot" executive functioning processes involve interpersonal and social tasks (McDonald, 2007; Stuss and Anderson, 2004; Stuss, Gallup and Alexander, 2001), and affective and motivational processing (Metcalfe and Mischel, 1999; Zelazo and Müller, 2002). According to Burack et al. (2010), emotionally related "hot" executive and regulatory processing has received far less attention in the research literature compared to the "cool" processes, and even less is understood about emotional regulation when both "hot" and "cool" systems are required.

Executive Functions and Speech–Language Pathology

Speech–language pathologists Richard and Fahy (2005) describe executive functioning as "the ability to anticipate consequences, generate novel solutions, initiate appropriate actions or responses to situations, monitor the ongoing success or failure of one's behavior, and modify performance based on unexpected changes" (p.13). Executive functioning components are important for developing plans for future actions, retaining these plans and action sequences in working memory until they are executed, and inhibiting irrelevant actions (Pennington and Ozonoff 1996). Executive functions described by Richard and Fahy (2005) are presented in Table 3.2.

While many speech–language pathologists (SLP) continue to treat ASD as a behavioral disorder, a growing number of SLPs, and especially ASD researchers, are recognizing that ASD is not a behavioral disorder but a cognitive disability. The observed characteristics are the result of extreme dysfunctions of executive functioning processes. Table 3.2 presents examples of impaired executive functioning. As can be seen, these are common among individuals with autism spectrum disorders.

Table 3.2 Impairments associated with deficits in executive functions

Communication
• Failure to process, comprehend, or recall instructions in their entirety; unable to recall details
• Failure to initiate requesting help, clarification, or repetition; unable to formulate on the spot
• Impulsive responses, interjections, or interruptions; unable to inhibit comments until appropriate
• Poor use of self-talk to consider plans, ponder potential outcomes, or prompt behaviors
• Disorganized, poorly planned syntax and cohesion, in both oral and written communication
• Failure to comprehend main theme or idea despite understanding specific words or sentences
Pragmatics and social interaction
• Poor ability to take others' perspective
• Poor shifting and adaptation to others' needs and perspectives
• Inattention to and/or failure to recognize nonverbal or subtle social cues
• Inaccurate judgement of situations
• Inappropriate, impulsive, or dangerous behavior
Reasoning
• Difficulty recognizing relevant versus irrelevant input
• Difficulty drawing conclusions and making inferences
• Limited abstract reasoning, affecting efforts to generate strategic plans
• Limited divergent thinking; poor ability to generate multiple options, possibilities, or ideas
• Limited ability to predict consequences or outcomes; cannot recognize nonstrategic options

cont.

Functional problem solving and new learning

- Impaired strategic thinking; may engage in futile attempts or simple, trial-and-error attempts
- Limited ability to generate multiple solutions; may persist with failed efforts
- Difficulty generalizing to other contexts; may be unable to see patterns or parallels
- Trouble learning from consequences
- May be context dependent and require cues again subsequent times
- Impaired ability to carry out instructions or tasks to completion; may become distracted, frustrated
- Impulsive attempts with failed outcomes, despite verbalizing appropriate intentions or plans
- Unable to recognize failure or the need to revise strategies

Memory

- Difficulty retaining information long enough to execute steps
- Forgetting to execute tasks or to be where necessary at a given time
- Recalling information out of sequential or temporal order, including verbal directions
- Failure to integrate long-term memories of past experiences into future decisions

Source: Richard and Fahy, 2005. Reproduced with permission.

CHAPTER 4

Impulse Control and Emotion Regulation

Where Stress Reactions Come From

Making complex decisions effectively requires giving ourselves at least a moment to think about what to choose or what to do, based on our current situation in relation to our world knowledge (prior learning). Complex decision-making requires (1) pausing and (2) reflecting. These are two distinct cognitive activities located in separate parts of the brain. Behan, Stone and Garavan (2015) refer to these as our impulsive system and our reflective system, which are activated, respectively, in the ventral striatum associate with reward gratification (McClure et al., 2004), and the prefrontal cortex associated with cognitive control (Dalley et al., 2007) (see Figure 4.1). Pausing requires that we inhibit activation of the ventral striatum (our impulsive system); reflecting requires that we activate the prefrontal cortex (our reflective system).

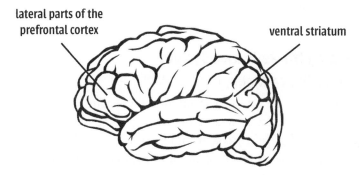

lateral parts of the prefrontal cortex

ventral striatum

Figure 4.1 The prefrontal cortex and ventral striatum

In contrast to complex decision-making, when stressed we typically make an impulsive choice to immediately relieve us from the immediate cause of the stress. Making an impulsive choice requires inhibiting controlled cognitive processes, and quickly responding to achieve a reward or avoid feeling stressed. Impulsive choice involves making a decision without forethought about possible consequences (Basar et. al., 2010). Conversely, reflective responding is activated if we are concerned about making an inappropriate response (Basar et al., 2010): that is, fear of making a mistake, and thereby delaying making an immediate decision while we weigh the alternatives. Thus, impulsivity is a multidimensional construct requiring both activation of the impulsive system and inhibition of the slower reflective system. This also reflects the dual nature of decision-making as related to both the limbic system (emotion; immediate gratification) and the more traditional problem-solving system of the prefrontal cortex.

For children with ASD, responding to a question asked by someone else is a form of dialogic interaction (Fernyhough, 1996), and is stressful. A child with ASD may begin "stimming," a behavioral response to unlabeled physiological discomfort the child feels (tightness in the gut, etc.) as a result of being stressed by the person asking the question. An immediate response, guessing, is one strategy the child may take. This is an example of impulsive choice-making—it is the first answer that comes into the child's mind—in the hope of ending the interaction and relieving the physiological feeling associated with having to answer the question. In this scenario the child's primary goal is not to answer the question correctly, but to end the questioning.

Activating the Reflective System
Teaching Choice-Making
Developing complex decision-making skills requires helping the child activate her reflective system, rather than to respond impulsively. This requires that the child *pause*, in order to *reflect* on the question, and choose the correct answer, or in more complex situations, make the least incorrect response.

To inhibit the child's impulsive responding when asked a question, as soon as the child begins to impulsively respond to a question, Janice will immediately raise her hand in front of the child, and say,

"STOP. Your brain needs five seconds to think about the question."

If the child has difficulty stopping, Janice might begin modeling what she wants ("One...two...three...four...five"), to help the child do her own counting, before answering the question. When teaching choice-making with younger children, Janice may hold up a stop sign, and then start the counting process with the child. This is done to inhibit the impulsive choice system in order to allow time for the reflective system to be activated.

The reflective process involves three cognitive processes.

1. *What should I be attending to?* This may be picking among a set of pictures, or picking among written choices or visual choices, or attending to a speaker who is asking the questions (auditory attention).

2. *What should I be thinking about?* This includes pulling possible options into working memory from long-term memory (world knowledge), and comparing and contrasting those with the information (or question) directly in front of me.

3. *What should I do,* that is, which of the options should I choose? If this is in response to a question from an adult, it means answering the question verbally. However, it might also be choosing a behavioral response in a social or emotional situation: do I hit the person, or walk away, or respond verbally, and so on.

Thus, what the adult may think is a straightforward question requires three sets of reflective choices: *what to attend to, what to think about* and *what to do,* each of which requires suppressing the impulsive choice reaction, which is the purpose of pausing and reflecting.

Inhibition Control and Learning

Inhibition control is also necessary for academic learning. Richland and Burchina (2013) found that both inhibition control and vocabulary knowledge *independently* contribute to children's scores on the Verbal Analogies subtest of the Woodcock-Johnson Psycho-Educational Battery—Revised (WJ-R; Woodcock and Johnson, 1990). In other words, language development alone is not sufficient for developing verbal analogy skills. Effective academic learning also requires developing executive functioning skills generally, and inhibition control ability specifically (Diamond and Lee, 2011).

Limitations in executive functioning have also been found to explain why scores on IQ tests often appear to decrease with age in children with ASD (Barneveld et al., 2014). High-level, more complex tasks for older children involve an increased emphasis on reasoning skills over rote memory or knowledge. Barneveld and colleagues found that children diagnosed with high-functioning autism who were six to eight years old performed at normal levels on IQ tests (mean = 103). However, groups of progressively older children diagnosed with high-functioning autism performed progressively more poorly on IQ tests; for example, children with an average age of 13 had, on average, IQ scores of 95. More importantly, these lower scores correlated with an ability to sustain attention and become distracted, as well as decreased fine motor abilities.

These findings have practical implications for parents, teachers and clinicians. Early-age IQ testing may not pick up existing neurocognitive difficulties such as those of young children with ASD. A "normal" IQ score could disqualify them for an Individual Education Plan (IEP) and intervention services at the very ages when these services have the greatest long-term effect. Moreover, the delay in receiving appropriate diagnoses and the concomitant IEPs set up these children to continue to be behind or require even greater intervention efforts, which are additionally stressful for these children, in order to catch up and keep up with other children their age.

Inhibitory Control, Anticipatory Anxiety, and the Insistence on Sameness

One of the hallmarks of autism is an insistence on sameness (IoS; Gray and Tonga, 2005; Sinha et al., 2014). Insistence on sameness is one of the diagnostic characteristics of autism listed in the DSM-5 (American Psychiatric Association, 2013).

Sinha et al. (2014) have posited that autism is a disorder of prediction. Individuals with ASD react to events or stimuli without consideration of their past experiences with similar events or stimuli—not taking into consideration past experiences results in an impairment in prediction. They hypothesize that predictive impairment in autism (PIA) may contribute to many of the diagnostic criteria exhibited by individuals with ASD, including social communication difficulties, repetitive behaviors (stimming), insistence on sameness, sensory hypersensitivities, reduced appreciation of humor, and difficulties with basic motion detection or other forms of moving objectives (e.g. driving), and theory of mind. As partial support for their hypotheses about PIA, they point to research showing that individuals with ASD have atypical development in the areas of the brain most associated with the ability to make predictions, the striatum, basal ganglia, anterior cingula, and cerebellum.

In essence, Sinha et al. (2014) are arguing that because individuals with ASD are not making predictions based on past experiences, they experience a chaotic world. The desire for sameness and well-defined rules is their means of making their world more predictable, and as a result less confusing and less stressful.

The implications of this are significant for predicting emotional responses or outbursts. If we cannot anticipate what is about to happen in the next moment, we are more likely to become anxious (Abott and Baddia, 1986; Herry et al., 2007). In neurotypical children, increased anxiety is often expressed physically by repetitive behaviors such as tapping toes, strumming fingers on a table, leg-swinging, and so on. These are examples of what we could call low-level stimming in the face of anxiety or frustration in neurotypical children. In individuals with ASD, their predictive ability is significantly diminished; their anxiety or frustration is greater, and therefore it is natural that stimming behavior will be more extreme. Insistence on sameness eliminates unpredictability, reduces the level of frustration and anxiety, and makes our ability to self-regulate in these situations easier.

Every moment we are awake, we are making moment-to-moment predictions. Some we make subconsciously or almost automatically. When someone enters a room, we immediately evaluate who that person is, and if we need to do something. Based on our past experiences, we make different predictions and therefore respond differently depending on whether it is a spouse, a parent, a child or a stranger. Seeing a familiar person in an unexpected situation, for example seeing a teacher in a clothing store versus in a classroom, stimulates both a physiological reaction (widening of the eyes, visceral response in the gut, etc.), as well as a more deliberate cognitive decision-making process. We will consciously pull from long-term memory into working memory past experiences, if any, of seeing that person outside of school, past situations with other people in this situation, for example the clothing store, and so on, and compare those with the current situation to decide what we should do (greet the person, ignore the person, talk about school, not talk about school, etc.). In other words we make predictions about what the best course of action to take is in this new situation. Without the ability to make moment-to-moment predictions, every event, every experience, every new person, and so on becomes a potential crisis. Making predictions provides us with a means of feeling in control of our environment.

To summarize, the ability to make predictions involves the same three-phase cognitive process described previously.

1. *What should I be attending to?* Knowing what to focus on in the current situation.

2. *What should I be thinking about?* Knowing which experiences from my past are relevant to the current situation.

3. *What should I do?* Knowing what response to choose in the existing situation.

For children with ASD, the insistence on sameness arguably reflects a subconscious desire to not become dysregulated. Having to make moment-to-moment predictions in order to make necessary decisions in response to anticipated problems that may arise in each novel situation involves a lot of cognitive effort, and is therefore very stressful. For these children, the inability to efficiently and reliably think about what to attend to, what to think about and what to do may lead to a subconscious semi-effective strategy, such as stimming, as an attempt to experience self-control or self-regulation in the situation.

Emotion Regulation

An emotional reaction to a situation evokes multiple reactions: *physiological*—adrenaline, tightening in the gut, increased heart rate, pupil dilation, and so on; a *subjective interpretation* in which a label is attached to an emotion—fear, joy, sadness, excitement, etc.; and *behavioral*—change in posture or facial expression, staring, screaming, hitting, running, and so on (Gross, 2014).

The relationship between emotions and any given situation is reciprocal: emotional reactions change in response to the situation that prompted them, and the situation changes in response to the reactions of the individual. For example, imagine a situation in which an adult poses a question to a child. The child has an unconscious, autonomic nervous system reaction resulting in a physiological response (adrenaline rush, increased heart rate, etc.), and an expressive reaction: change of posture, eyes widening, and so on. Depending on how and how quickly the adult responds to these expressions, the child will respond accordingly. A threatening voice will result in a heightened physiological response which in turn stimulates an even more expressive reaction; a calm voice can inhibit the physiological response and likely reduce the expressive reaction.

To help children with ASD manage their emotions, it is useful to consider emotional regulation in the context of a situational process. The emotional regulation process was described by Gross (1998), and applied to individuals with ASD by Weiss, Thomson and Chan (2014). Referred to as the *modal model of emotion regulation* (Gross and Thompson, 2007), it involves five linked domains or "families" of emotion regulation, which result in different strategies for gaining or maintaining emotion regulation:

- situation selection
- situation modification
- attentional deployment
- cognitive change
- response modulation.

Parents or caretakers of individuals with ASD often undertake one or more of these strategies to manage emotional outbursts in their children with ASD. As a therapist, my goal is to help children develop their own strategies for self-regulation.

Situation selection involves "understanding a specific situation, predicting its probable outcomes, and evaluating the consequences of entering into it adaptively (e.g. avoiding potentially dangerous situations) or maladaptively (e.g. persistently avoiding reasonably safe situations)" (Weiss et al., 2014, pp.630–631). The executive functions that are required to do this are difficult for individuals with ASD. It involves making predictions, comparing and contrasting, and deciding what to do; it requires the child to pause, plan and reflect.

Situation modification requires modifying a situation in order to alter its emotional impact. What may appear as obsessive desire for sameness is an example of modifying a situation in order to reduce hyper-stimulation and maintain emotional control. Temple Grandin, the internationally known writer and researcher who has high-functioning autism, putting herself into her "squeeze box" is an example of her modifying her situation to control the overstimulation she was experiencing:

> I constructed [a squeeze box] to satisfy my craving for the feeling of being held. The machine was designed so that I could control the amount and duration of the pressure. It was lined with foam rubber and applied pressure over a large area of my body. Gradually I was able to tolerate the machine holding me. The oversensitivity of my nervous system was slowly reduced. A stimulus that was once overwhelming and aversive had now become pleasurable. Using the machine enabled me to tolerate another person touching me. (Grandin, 1996, p.3)

Attentional deployment is directing attention within a given situation towards or away from the source of emotional dysregulation in order to influence one's emotions. Children with ASD will often direct their attention away from a source of dysregulation (looking away from a teacher who is asking difficult questions), or may become obsessed with a source of stimulation and be unable to focus away from it.

Cognitive change "refers to modifying how one appraises a situation so as to alter its emotional significance, either by changing how one thinks about the situation or about one's capacity to manage the demands it poses" (Gross, 2014, p.10). Children with ASD often see situations as all-or-nothing or engage in end-of-the-world thinking.

Response modulation "involves the continuum of physiological and behavioral ways of regulating and expressing emotions after they are experienced" (Weiss et al., 2014, p.631). The most common example of this in individuals with ASD is stimming. Children with ASD stim as a way to control their sense of overstimulation.

CHAPTER 5

Implicit Learning

Explicit learning is the conscious process we use to acquire new knowledge or new skills. What teachers do in classrooms, the teaching strategies they use to structure information to make it most understandable, are designed to facilitate explicit learning. Likewise, when individuals actively seek out the structure of information presented to them they are explicitly learning.

In contrast, implicit learning is a passive process. Individuals learn by exposure to new information, situations, and so on, and at a subconscious level learn without actively being taught. All neurotypical children and adults do this naturally. Implicit learning is learning that takes place without conscious effort (Klinger et al., 2006). Social engagement rules are examples of rules that are learned implicitly. Implicit social engagements rules tell us *why* we should act in a certain way, not simply *what* to do: *if* we want someone to like us, *then* we need to show them we like them too. Neurotypical children will see a peer get praise from the teacher for quietly sitting in his seat. They will learn without being taught that they are more likely to be liked by their teacher if they sit quietly in their seat. More importantly, they implicitly infer this "quiet rule" and apply it to other situations— other teachers in other classrooms and other adults at the dinner table or other situations. No one explicitly taught them to apply this rule to other people and other situations; they learned it implicitly. Implicit learning is how we learn to *apply* knowledge or rules to new situations.

Unfortunately, children with ASD have neurocognitive impairments that limit their ability to learn implicitly (Klinger et al., 2006). Children with ASD do not realize that not acknowledging someone else sends the message to the other person that they do not want to interact with the other person. Children with ASD have problems making friends because they are not able to learn *implicitly* the social interaction rules needed to make friends. Thus context is important: it is not sufficient to teach simply what needs to be done, for example when someone says hello, you need to say hello back. It is important to know the *why* behind the rule: that is, to show someone we like him. Explicitly teaching the *why* behind a social interaction is critical for generalizing authenticity—*I am doing this because I want to show you I like you*, rather than *I am doing it because the rule is to say "hello" when someone else says "hello."*

Explicit teaching of social skills tends to have a limited carryover/generalization to everyday experiences because applying and using a rule or skill is learned *implicitly* not explicitly. This is exemplified in the box below, The *Getting a cookie* rule versus the *Getting what I want* rule. In the cookie example, the neurotypical child was taught an explicit rule, and implicitly knew to apply it to other situations: she learned that asking politely was a means of getting what she wanted. The child with autism was taught the same explicit rule, but because of how autism limits her cognitive processing, she did not implicitly think to generalize the rule to other problem-solving situations. Instead, she learned the more specific *Getting a cookie* rule.

Implicit learning is also the basis of cognitive categorization—the formation of cognitive categories that are a critical part of abstract thinking, generalization, and efficient processing and storing of new information. Klinger et al. (2006), used an example provided by Temple Grandin of how her understanding of "cat" is different than that of neurotypicals (Grandin, 1995, p.142). Unlike neurotypicals, whose "cat concept" might be something like "furry animals with eyes facing front, have whiskers, and so on," Grandin describes how she had to memorize different examples of cats, like a "series of videos," and then consciously (explicitly) collect them into a cognitive category. Neurotypicals, when seeing a lion, tiger, puma or cheetah, would immediately recognize these as part of the "cat category," and would implicitly create a new subcategory: BIG cats. In contrast, Grandin, unless told they were cats, might not automatically see them as part of the cat category, or would need to effortfully think about other cats and possibly make the conclusion that these are also cats.

THE *GETTING A COOKIE* RULE VERSUS THE *GETTING WHAT I WANT* RULE

What the neurotypical child learns

A young neurotypical child wants a cookie; her plan is to scream and yell until she gets it. But instead of getting the cookie, she is put in "time out." She learns that yelling and screaming does not get her a cookie, but other strategies, for example politely asking her mother for a cookie, gets her the cookie. More importantly, she learns implicitly that by politely asking for something rather than yelling and screaming she can get what she wants. She has learned the *Getting what I want* rule.

What the ASD child learns

A young girl with autism also wants a cookie; her plan is to scream and yell until she gets it. But instead of getting a cookie, she is put in "time out." But her mother explains to her that if instead of yelling and screaming she politely asks for the cookie, her mom will give her a cookie. Her mother has explicitly taught her daughter that being polite will get her a cookie. And that is exactly what the child with autism learns: that the way to get a cookie is to ask politely. And the next time she wants a cookie, she politely asks her mom for one, and she gets a cookie. Unfortunately because of the way her brain processes information, the daughter with autism is not able to generalize this naturally to other things she wants. She is not able to implicitly apply the rule to other things she wants. The daughter has learned only the more specific *Getting a cookie* rule.

The ability to implicitly (automatically) categorize information is essential for learning (Reber, 1989). It is how we cognitively process information, and how we develop abstract thinking. Klinger et al. (2006) argue that because individuals with ASD are unable to do this implicitly, explicit instruction may be necessary to compensate for implicit learning impairments.

Another example of implicit learning is what is known as incidental learning. Much of early childhood language development is implicit; it takes place in the everyday environment of the child. The cognitive process of "fast mapping" allows a young child to hear a word once or perhaps twice and store it in long-term memory for later use.

"FAST MAPPING" AND LANGUAGE DEVELOPMENT IN INFANTS

Infants begin learning language via fast mapping. They just need to hear a word once to have an understanding of the word. For example, when an adult points to a dog and the infant looks in that direction, and the adult immediately says, "Look, there's a dog," the infant begins to understand the association of the label "dog" with the animal. The child may not yet be able to say the word "dog," but the child understands what "dog" refers to. When asked, "Where is the dog?" the infant will point to the dog.

Another common example is when an adult asks an infant, "Where's your nose?" or "Where's your ear?" As an adult, we don't expect the child to say the word, but to understand the label and point to his nose or ear. These are examples of language development through fast mapping.

Toddlers learn grammatical rules implicitly by listening to others, such as their parents or older siblings, and somehow automatically process them cognitively. Young children implicitly learn the grammatical rule *add "ed" to a verb to change the tense*. As parents, we know they have learned this rule when they apply it irregular verbs, and say "bringed" instead of "brought." In contrast, an explicit language rule is *i before e, except after c*. When we apply this rule to spelling, we are doing so consciously, not implicitly (Klinger et al., 2006).

CHAPTER 6

The *Thinking in Speech* Model of Reasoning and Problem-Solving

Problem-solving has been described as the most complex of all intellectual functions (Goldstein and Levin, 1987). Problem-solving is "goal-directed" cognitive activity (Rath et al., 2003, p.137) that is required in new situations, that is, in situations where the individual has no prior experience (Luria, 1966; Sohlbert and Mateer, 2001). Problem-solving occurs in every new situation, not just when an individual is faced with an education problem, or a work-related problem, or some other technical problem. Social interactions also require problem-solving. D'Zurilla and Maydeu-Olivares (1995) refer to this as social problem-solving, which includes interactions with parents, teachers, friends, family members, clinicians, and so on.

Problems in everyday situations tend to be obscure and complex (Rath et al., 2003). They require higher-level cognition, that is, executive functioning. As noted by Channon (2004), "New problems crop up unexpectedly and in less-than-ideal circumstances, and there may be little time to ponder them and consider the merits of alternative approaches" (p.236).

Executive functioning processes include planning, working memory, cognitive flexibility, and so on. When applied to traditional problem-solving tasks, such as education problems, work-related problems, and most neuropsychological measures, these can be referred to as "cool" executive functioning processing (Burack et al., 2010), as opposed to "hot" executive functioning processes, which involve interpersonal and social tasks (see Chapter 3 for an explanation of "hot" and "cool" executive functioning processes) (McDonald, 2007; Stuss and Anderson, 2004; Stuss et al., 2001), and affective and motivational processing (Metcalfe and Mischel, 1999; Zelazo and Müller, 2002). Cognitively, solving real-world problems requires both "hot" and "cool" executive functioning processes (Zelazo and Müller, 2002). According to Burack et al. (2010), emotionally related "hot" executive and regulatory processing has received far less attention in the research literature compared to the "cool" processes, and even less is understood about emotional regulation when both "hot" and "cool" systems are required.

Executive functioning disorders are common in children with ASD (Zenko, 2014). Thus, it is not surprising that children with ASD have difficulty with social interactions that require "hot" executive functioning. As will be emphasized throughout this book, when children with ASD have difficulty in social interactions with parents, teachers, other children, and so on, these are not behavioral problems, but executive functioning problems. Thus, successful treatment should focus on treating the child's inability to apply a problem-solving strategy related to her underlying executive functioning disorder, rather than misattribute the problems to some form of "anti-social" or attention-seeking behavior.

Inner Speech: How We Use Language to Reason and Problem-Solve

"In his early observation of children's language, Piaget (1923/1959) described a type of speech which appeared to have no communicative function and which he took to reflect the young child's egocentrism" (Fernyhough, 2010, p.65). This non-communicative speech is now referred to as "inner speech." Inner speech plays an important role in self-regulation (Fernyhough, 2010), as well as in higher-level thinking: reasoning and problem-solving (Akbar, Loomis and Paul, 2013; Whitehouse, Mayberry and Durkin, 2006; Williams et al., 2012).

According to Vygotsky (1987 [1934]), the ability to "think in speech" is critical for flexible behavior and cognition, and is the foundation for effective self-regulation. Verbal thinking has its roots in linguistically mediated exchanges with others (such as caregivers) early in life (Vygotsky, 1987 [1934]). These interpersonal dialogues serve as an externally driven means of regulating the child's behavior early in life. Gradually, interpersonal speech becomes intrapersonal speech, and the child is able to regulate her own behavior by engaging in a dialogue within her self in the absence of others (Barkley, 1997). This internal verbal or linguistic thinking has been labeled *inner speech* (Vygotsky, 1986).

Charles Fernyhough was among the first to suggest that individuals with ASD would be expected to show diminished tendencies to employ inner speech as a primary means of thinking (Fernyhough, 1996, 2009). Subsequent research confirmed that individuals with ASD had diminished or underdeveloped language skills (Akbar et al., 2013) and inner speech (Whitehouse et al., 2006; Williams et al., 2012). While difference in the ability to use inner speech between typical children and children with ASD is now well documented, according to Williams et al. (2012, p.237), "no such [inner speech] training efforts have been targeted at children with ASD, [and]…there may be some value to conducting studies to explore this issue further." *Thinking in Speech* is, to our knowledge, the first intervention designed specifically to develop "inner speech." Our goal is to help children with ASD use inner speech to improve their independent problem-solving and emotional regulation.

Self-Regulation: Social Problem-Solving Applied to One's Self

Ochsner and Gross (2005) describe self-regulation as the thought process used to control emotion in stress-inducing situations. Self-regulation, like other forms of executive functioning, depends on some form of linguistic thinking (e.g. Baldo et al., 2005; Gruber and Goschke, 2004; Williams et al., 2012). For example, Barkley (1997) observed that children with attention deficit/hyperactivity disorder (ADHD) were slower to develop internalized speech than typically developing children, and had difficulty with aspects of executive functioning and self-regulation. Hrabok and Kerns (2010), citing Barkley (1997), state, "following the development of internalized speech, children are able to make use of increasingly complex rules, and the child's internalization of these rules and use of 'private speech' translates into improved self-control and regulation and increasingly internalized control of behavior" (p.146). Thus, the definition of social problem-solving must include both interpersonal and intrapersonal problem-solving (Rath et al., 2003): respectively, interactions with someone else, and interactions with one's self.

Since executive functioning disorders are common in children with ASD (Zenko, 2014), we would expect children with ASD who can develop internalized speech not only to improve their problem-solving ability, but also to have improved self-control and regulation.

Helping Children with ASD Develop and Use an Independent Problem-Solving Strategy

Cognitive and language profiles of children with ASD present differently with respect to their unique abilities to express thoughts and feelings and deal effectively with stressful situations (Bialystock et al., 2003; Just et al., 2007). In general, however, for children with ASD, linguistic thinking—using language to solve a complex problem—can create an emotional paradox. They need to use language to "talk themselves through" the emotional feeling—stress—associated with solving difficult tasks (Miyake et al., 2004), yet the inability to use language skills to talk themselves through a difficult task, and the related emotional feelings, create more stress. Thus helping these children use language to solve complex problems is not sufficient; they simultaneously need to be taught how to cope with the emotional stress associated with solving challenging tasks.

This intervention helps the child engage in three problem-solving steps necessary for maintaining emotional regulation in order to solve higher-order problems: (1) recognize that they are feeling stress because they are in a problem-solving situation; (2) retrieve possible strategies that could solve this problem; and (3) verbalize the chosen strategy to the clinician.

Step 1: Recognizing that one is in a problem-solving situation

In everyday social problem-solving situations, recognizing that one is entering a problem situation is typically cued by a physiological feeling, for example, a tightening of the stomach, or as a cognitive feeling such as a rush of uncontrollable thoughts, or as an emotional feeling such as fear. The emotional/motivational input is referred to as a somatic marker (Damasio, Everitt and Bishop, 1996); it is the nonspecific "feeling" associated with a future outcome. "A child must attend to internal information (e.g. level of comfort, distress, etc.), contextual information (e.g. who is present in the environment), and social cues from others in determining the most appropriate course of action" (Hrabok and Kerns, 2010, p.145). Explicit statements help the child with ASD attend to internal information. Landry et al. (2002) found that using language to label and guide actions had a direct influence on language development and nonverbal problem-solving at age four. Thus, when working with children with ASD, the clinician must explicitly help the child recognize the same information cues.

To facilitate the development of Step 1, recognizing the onset of a problem-solving situation, the clinician helps the child with ASD to recognize the cues the child needs to attend to when starting to feel stressed. The clinician must be explicit. For example, when the clinician asks the child a challenging question, the clinician should look for signs of stress (fidgeting, putting her head down on the table, monologuing, etc.), and immediately and explicitly point out what the child is doing that implies she is entering into a problem situation ("Your closing your eyes tells me that…"), and also explain that this is what learning feels like ("This is what learning feels like; learning is hard").

Our recommendation with children with ASD is to be simple and explicit. Often a teacher, clinician or caregiver will refer to learning as "sometimes hard" or "can be hard." "Sometimes" and "can be" are context-dependent in that how challenging any given situation will feel varies. Children with ASD are black-and-white thinkers. Something is either "hard" or "not hard." They don't have the shades of gray, so initially, the adult has to give the child a concrete label and example. For example, "Reading is hard for me. This is what learning feels like. Once I practice, I get to call it 'easy.' My brain has a hard time with reading words. This is what learning to read feels like. The only way I get to call it 'easy' is to practice. Once I practice. It will feel easier." (Teaching "shades of gray" is discussed in Chapter 8, "Developing Mental and Emotions Vocabulary.")

Step 2: Realizing a strategy to solve the problem and ease stress

For the second component, the child must realize a strategy that will solve the problem and ease the stress. The ill-defined nature of many everyday life problems means that all the relevant information needed for problem-solving is rarely available; this contrasts sharply with more typical laboratory-based problems that have well-defined structures (Galotti, 1989). As noted by Channon and Crawford (1999, p.757), "Successful solution involves appreciation not only of the actual facts of the [everyday] problem situation [hot executive functioning], but of all the pertinent issues taking into consideration the motivations and sensibilities of the people involved, the practicalities, and the potential consequences of possible courses of action [cool executive functioning]."

For children with ASD, coping with problem-solving situations that require simultaneous hot (planning, working memory, cognitive flexibility, etc.) and cool (interpersonal and social tasks) cognitive processing can be challenging. A problem-solving strategy that engages the hot and cool aspects of executive functioning is independently asking for help. Asking for help requires separating one's self (thoughts, knowledge and feelings) from the other person; that is, it requires theory of mind (Baron-Cohen, Leslie and Frith, 1985; Miller, 2006). To ask for help, a child must first recognize that another person knows things or can do things that are different from his- or herself (Fahy, 2014; Harris, de Rosnay and Pons, 2005). Developing theory of mind is especially difficult for children with ASD (Baron-Cohen, 2000; Pellicano, 2007).

As with Step 1, Step 2 can require prompting by the clinician. For example, after telling the child "this is what hard feels like; this is what learning feels like" (Step 1 prompt), the clinician should then state, "You are showing me you need help. When I hear 'I need help,' I can help you" (Step 2 prompt). This prompt is explicit; the clinician is providing the child with a strategy, asking for help, that can address the source of the stress, and thereby reduce the likelihood of emotional dysregulation. It is also helping the child understand that what she ("self") is experiencing is not necessarily understood by the clinician ("other"), that is, theory of mind.

Step 3: Verbalizing the strategy

Finally, the third component in the development of the child's problem-solving ability is verbalizing[1] the strategy in response to the problem. Explicitly articulating the strategy is also important for developing working memory and long-term memory (Baddeley, 2003; Hoskyn, 2010). Requiring the child to verbally express asking for help requires engaging in an interpersonal dialogue. This is the precursor to true inner speech. Inner speech is critical for flexible behavior and cognition, and is the foundation for effective self-regulation (Vygotsky, 1987 [1934]). Parents use interpersonal dialogues to regulate children's behavior. Over time, children internalize these dialogues. Eventually, children are able to regulate their own behavior by engaging in a dialogue within themselves in the absence of others (Barkley, 1997). Interpersonal dialogue becomes intrapersonal dialogue. Requiring the child to use language explicitly to solve a problem is intended to be the child's the first step towards eventual inner speech.

Inner Speech: From Developmental Model to Clinical Intervention

True thinking as inner speech is more than simply an internalized verbalization of private speech or an isomorphic representation of a dialogue with someone else. Fernyhough (2004) refers to this as condensed inner speech, where thoughts are abbreviated forms of sentences with more expansive meaning beyond simple definitions. We would argue that this expanded meaning includes the "meaning within the context" where context is both that in the present as well as the past experiences of the individual. This also includes any emotional context that exists based on the individual's past experiences.

---

1   While we use "verbalizing," "verbalize," "verbalization," or "verbally" throughout this paper, we do not limit this to only oral speech. Nonverbal children can use augmented speech devices. Our point is not that the strategy needs to be oral, but that the child must explicitly express the strategy in order to develop linguistically mediated exchanges.

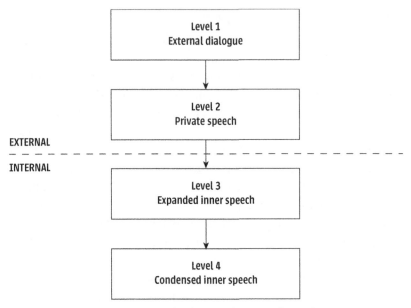

Figure 6.1 Levels of internalization of speech
Adapted, with permission, from Fernyhough, 2004.

Fernyhough (2004) presents a four-level process for thinking about Vygotsky's description of the internalization of external speech to inner speech. Level 1 is *external dialogue*. External dialogue refers to overt dialogues that take place between people. Level 2 is *private speech*. Private speech is self-talk; it is the dialogue that the child has with herself, sometimes out loud and sometimes as a subvocalization. Level 3 is *expanded inner speech*. Expanded inner speech is private speech that is fully internalized. It is "expanded" because it maintains the full conversational structure of a dialogue, but in this case the child is talking silently to herself. Finally is Level 4, *condensed inner speech*. Condensed inner speech is the "thinking as pure meaning" described by Vygotsky (Fernyhough, 2004), which includes the more expansive meanings associated with the situations and the individual's past experiences. The normal developmental process of internalization described by Fernyhough is presented in Figure 6.1. Fernyhough notes that in times of demanding cognitive conditions these steps may be reversed. For example, during complex problem-solving, an individual may revert from condensed inner speech to expanded inner speech (thinking in full sentences) or even to vocalized private speech. Similar reverse internalization may occur during times of stress.

Fernyhough (1996, 2009, 2010) distinguishes between two forms of verbalizations, dialogic and monologic. Dialogic refers to the form of verbal thinking that involves using language to analyze distinct perspectives of reality. Examples of dialogic problem-solving include comparing and contrasting choices, generating multiple possible solutions to a given problem, or comparing one's own perspective with that of someone else. In contrast, monologic speech is where a person focuses on one thing or one particular state of affairs. In this regard, monologic speech is comparable to stuck-in-set perseverance (Boucugnani and Jones 1989; Sandson and Albert 1984). When faced with a problem-solving situation, getting "stuck in set" can increase stress; the child may realize the "set" does not address the problem, but has no alternative language-based problem-solving strategy to break out of the monologue. Emotional dysregulation may result.

Monologic speech is common among children with ASD. Typical monologic speech is directive. That is, while it has the appearance of an interpersonal interaction, the verbalizations, whether statements or questions, are directed at the listener but without necessarily an expectation or intention of a true dialogue. In contrast, a dialogic interaction, a true dialogue, requires each party in the interaction to pause and reflect about what the other person has said before responding. Reflecting on what the other person said requires language skills to think about the other person's perspective: theory of mind.

The *Thinking in Speech* intervention is intended to develop the child's inner speech. We, in effect, apply the steps of Fernyhough's developmental process, but do so explicitly and intentionally through interactive dialogic conversations with the child. The clinician uses the activities to engage in back-and-forth dialogues: Level 1 external dialogues. By teaching the child to "talk to your brain" the clinician is helping the child develop Level 2, private speech. Over time, the clinician helps the child transition to Level 3, expanded inner speech, by talking about circumstances that happen to the child, either in sessions or outside with others, when the child should be using self-talk rather than talking out loud. For example, when stressed and frustrated with the clinician, it is okay to think—to say in one's head—"I hate you right now!" but not to say it out loud to the clinician (or teacher or parent). Finally, complex problem-solving involves applying mental-state vocabulary to feelings in situations, using in-depth vocabulary knowledge or applying prior knowledge and comparing and contrasting situations and experiences (Level 4, compressed inner speech).

While all speech therapies are intended to increase verbalizations generally, *Thinking in Speech* focuses specifically on dialogic speech: asking the child questions that will cause the child emotional dysregulation (Step 1); require the child to consider a problem-solving strategy to solve the problem and ease the source of stress (Step 2); and finally require the child to verbalize the solution to the problem posed by the clinician (Step 3).

The *Thinking in Speech* Model for Developing Problem-Solving Ability

The *Thinking in Speech* clinical intervention builds six cognitive skills essential for language-based problem-solving: choice-making, using previously learned knowledge, in-depth vocabulary knowledge, pausing and reflecting, asking for help, and emotional and mental state vocabulary. These are shown in Figure 6.2, and described below. However, the clinical intervention does not focus on developing these as unique goals. Rather, these are executive functions that are activated during a clinical session.[2] Each activity during a session is an opportunity for the clinician to ensure that the child is activating her brain in such a way that any one or more of these components is required. Examples of how the clinician activates these components are presented in Chapters 7–13.

- *Choice-making:* A critical component of problem-solving is the ability to hold on to two or more pieces of information while at the same time comparing and contrasting one's choices *before* making a final decision (Hill, 2004; Vosniadou and Brewer, 1987).

- *Using previously learned knowledge:* Previously learned knowledge is developed by personal experiences and watching/listening to others. In addition to choice-making, a child needs to activate world knowledge (experiences the child has encountered), and compare and contrast the choice that was made with her life

---

2   Or for a parent, these are components that need to be activated during their 1:1 interactions with the child.

experiences, in order to decide on a logical response to the current situation or problem (Aro et al., 2014; Gillespie-Lynch et al., 2012; McGregor and Bean, 2012).

- *In-depth vocabulary knowledge:* Typical children learn, store and use novel vocabulary after one or two exposures to the word. This is known as "fast mapping." After the initial exposure, typical children gain a more in-depth understanding of vocabulary during their daily experiences. For example, the word "close," as in, "My neighbor lives close by," will have different meanings to different children depending on their world knowledge. Children who live in rural areas will have a different understanding of the concept of a "close neighbor" to children growing up in New York City (Gershkoff-Stowe and Hahn, 2007).

- *Pausing and reflecting:* Making complex decisions requires the ability to pause and think about our choices in relation to our world knowledge and current situation. Responding with no pausing or repeating the last thing one has heard are examples of a limited ability to stop and think about novel information (Fahy, 2014).

- *Asking for help:* The ability to understand what a problem "feels" like (e.g. a sensation of tightening in the stomach), and recognizing that when there is a problem that is unable to be independently resolved then assistance is required, is a very abstract concept that requires all of the above-listed components (Shaheen, 2014; Singer and Bashir, 1999; Ward and Jacobsen, 2014).

- *Emotional and mental state vocabulary* (learning the "shades of gray" in between the black and white): Verbs such as "think, know, believe" are considered mental state verbs as they describe thoughts and not actions. Children with ASD typically have difficulty developing vocabulary related to emotions and mental states. This includes learning alternative labels for emotions of varying intensity (Baron-Cohen, Golan and Ashwin, 2009; Capps, Yirmiya, and Sigman, 1992). In order to increase self-regulation, or what are known as "coping skills," one has to understand that the category "mad" has many different degrees, for example annoyed, frustrated or enraged. Each emotion word will have a different type of response, depending on the degree (Harris, Rosnay and Pons, 2005).

Through their use of inner speech, the child is able to think about how to solve a problem. Solving a problem requires applying one or more of the above cognitive skills. Carry-over occurs because the child is learning a problem-solving process that requires the brain to be activated broadly, simultaneously engaging both logical processes that are activated primarily in the prefrontal cortex of the brain, as well as the emotion-laden processes that reflect activation of the amygdala and the entire limbic system.

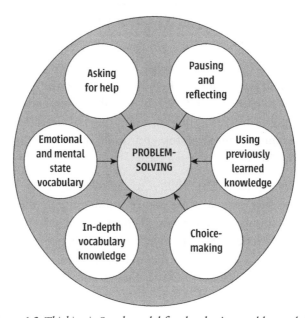

Figure 6.2 *Thinking in Speech* model for developing problem-solving

An abbreviated example: The fidgety child

When the child demonstrates emotional dysregulation (e.g. fidgeting, turning away), the clinician not only expresses what is going on (Steps 1 and 2)—"Uh oh, your brain is stuck. You are showing me you need help. When I hear 'I need help,' I can help you"—but then must wait for a fully verbalized response: "Miss Janice, I need help." If the child nods, the clinician can either not respond to the nod, or can prompt verbalization by modeling the targeted response expected of the child: "Miss Janice, I need help."[3]

Asking for help is an especially complex problem-solving strategy. It requires separating one's self (thoughts, knowledge and feelings) from the other person; that is, it requires theory of mind (Baron-Cohen, Leslie and Frith, 1985; Miller, 2006). To ask for help, children must first recognize that another person knows things or can do things that are different from themselves (Fahy, 2014; Harris et al., 2005). Developing theory of mind is especially difficult for children with ASD (Baron-Cohen, 2000; Pellicano, 2007). Finally, the child must express the strategy verbally. As noted previously, the outward expression of the strategy to the clinician is the precursor to private speech, where the child talks out loud to his- or herself, which in turn is the precursor to inner speech.

---

3   Note that the length of the request utterance will depend on the child's expressive language ability.

Part III

DEVELOPING INNER SPEECH FOR PROBLEM-SOLVING AND SOCIAL INTERACTIONS

I think therefore I am.

René Descartes, 1637

CHAPTER 7

Setting the Stage for the *Thinking in Speech* Intervention

Whether as a child or as an adult, learning is work. An adult in learning mode, that is, trying to process new information, often jokingly makes a comment like "This is giving me a headache," or "I just hit the wall." The child, including a neurotypical child, often responds differently. He becomes fidgety, or puts his head on the desk as if to go to sleep, or complains, "I'm tired of this" or "I don't want to do this anymore," or other phrases of frustration. Learning something new requires that our brains expend energy in order to actively process new information. It is tiring; it is not necessarily fun; it is more like work. Just as engaging in physical therapy after an injury requires extra physical effort, learning requires extra mental effort.

Because individuals with ASD have underconnectivity in their brain's frontal lobe (see Chapter 2), the information center of the brain, learning something new is especially hard. By definition, this is especially true in a learning situation, such as school, or during speech–language therapy. As a result, compared to neurotypical individuals, individuals with ASD must expend extra effort for problem-solving. As a parent, teacher or therapist, we need to recognize that when we place the child in a learning situation, we are requiring the child to work his brain.

In my first session, the goal is to understand the child's readiness to engage in effortful problem-solving. By the end of the first session, I hope to have answers to the following questions, which give me a sense of how to proceed.

- Does the child view himself as a learner, as opposed to feeling helpless in a learning situation?

- What is the child's understanding of what a problem feels like?

- How does the child respond when faced with a problem or question?

  - does he remain relatively calm, and respond with an independently derived answer, or

  - does he shut down or become emotionally dysregulated?

Introducing the "Brain Teacher"

I begin my first session by introducing myself as a "brain teacher" and explain why the child is with me. Being the child's "brain teacher" helps me: (1) build trust between the child and me, and (2) build the child's self-esteem and self-confidence as an independent problem-solver. I explain to the child,

> "You are here to become the boss of your brain—so grown-ups don't have to 'bug' you all the time."

Then, to show the child what "bugging" means, I will bombard him with instructions:

> "Give me the answer."

> "Let me do that for you."

Then I will ask,

> "How did that feel?" [The child will respond, "Bad."]

Then I state,

> "That's right. That's what we call 'bugging.'"

Then I will explain to the child in an encouraging voice:

> "You are going to show grown-ups that they do not have to bug you anymore.
>
> You're going to show everyone how smart, fun and wonderful you are.
>
> When you start showing everyone you are the boss of your brain, you don't need to come here anymore."

This introduction serves two key purposes. First, it explains why the child is in my room. Second, it helps the child get ready for working on activities and topics that will be challenging and feel stressful.

"Are You Smart?"

The first thing I ask the child after explaining that I will be his brain teacher, is:

"Are you smart?"

For the child to become an independent problem-solver, he has to believe that he is a smart learner. Moreover, I want the child to know that I recognize that he is smart. When I ask the child, "Are you smart?" In general, the *only* answer I will accept is a verbal or augmented verbal response, "Yes, I am smart." I do not allow the child to answer the question by nodding; I need to hear a verbal response of some sort. Similarly, I listen to hear if he is impulsively answering with a fast "Yes" rather than taking a moment to think before responding. Impulsive responding to a question with a single word, "yes" or "no," is a common problem-solving strategy for a child with ASD. When the child nods or gives the one-word "yes" response, he is not truly owning that he is a smart learner. Instead the child has adopted a form of problem-solving that has often worked in the past, which is to automatically give a "yes" response to please adults. The child is using the "Make the clinician happy so she stops bugging me" problem-solving strategy. He wants the adult to stop bugging him; the child has "learned" to give a quick answer, for example "Yes," so that is what the child provides. In most cases, the child has learned that usually adults want affirming answers—"Yes"—so that is what he provides. Conversely, if the child sees in the adult's expression or words that he gave the wrong answer, the child will quickly change his response to "no." The child's personal goal is not in solving the problem posed by the adult, but rather to solve the "How do I get the adult to stop asking me questions?" problem.

When I ask a child, "Are you smart?" I also make the child *wait* (pause) before answering. Making the child pause before he responds gives the brain time to process the thoughts needed to think about the question instead of impulsively responding. As a clinician, I need to help the child to internalize his answer ("I am smart"). Believing in himself will be an important part of being ready to learn. A child who does not think of himself as smart is not likely to be motivated to work on activities that are challenging or stressful. Developing an intrinsic belief that "I am smart" is ultimately what we want the child to internalize—that he is in fact smart. Believing in oneself is critical to becoming an independent problem-solver.

Sometimes the child will not respond at all. This is *not* defiance; I am asking the child to respond in a way that is different than what he has done in the past (i.e. based on the child's previously learned knowledge). After waiting approximately five to ten seconds, if the child has not responded, I will turn my ear to the child, showing I am ready to listen. Typically the child will eventually whisper or say in a soft voice, "I am smart." Over time, as the child's self-esteem increases, I will hear the child state the response in a determined intonation rather than a whisper or questioning intonation. I want the child to view my therapy room as a safe space, where he has permission to take risks.

Making My Room a Safe Place

To help the child feel safe in my therapy room, I will verbally explain to him:

> "This is a practice room. There is no wrong way to do anything here. Nobody's brain is perfect. Everybody makes mistakes, every day.
>
> I make mistakes.
>
> Mom makes mistakes.
>
> Dad makes mistakes.
>
> Every boy and girl in your school makes mistakes.
>
> Even teachers make mistakes.
>
> Every person on the planet makes mistakes!
>
> But we all know how to 'show trying.' In my room when you show trying and you make a mistake, it's always okay. It is always okay to show trying. The trick is, to make different mistakes every time."

I use this "mistake" template often (e.g. "I make mistakes," "Mom makes mistakes," etc.). As the therapy proceeds over time, the questions and problems will become more challenging for the child. The one constant throughout will be that he knows it is okay to make mistakes as long as the child "shows trying," because "'showing trying' is showing how smart you are."

Helping the Child Become "The Boss of His Brain"

An important part of my therapy is helping the child learn that he is in control of his brain. I begin this process by showing a picture of the brain; I want the child to think of his brain like other parts of the body, something that the child can control. I help the child learn to separate "the brain" from the "the child." Only when the child can differentiate himself from his brain can the child actively become *the boss of his brain*. I start by taking out a simple line drawing of the brain, and a box of crayons with many colors. I point to the front part of the brain (the frontal lobe), and tell the child,

> "This is the part of your brain I'm going to teach you to be the boss of, and to talk to."

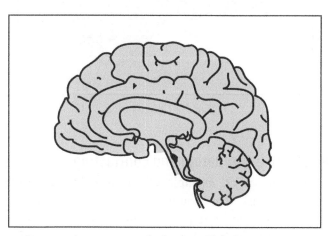

Figure 7.1 Simple drawing of the brain

Then, pointing to the rest of the brain, I will say,

> "We need the rest of the brain, but that's not the part I'm going to teach you to talk to and be the boss of."

For a younger child (preschool through early primary grades), I will show him a box of crayons and tell the child, "Take two crayons and color your brain." I have the child color the front part of the brain (the frontal lobe) a different color from the rest of the brain. If a child hesitates before starting, I will tell him, "There is no wrong way to do this." I explicitly praise throughout the coloring: "What great coloring you're doing!" "I like the color [green]—What a great choice!" "Let me know when you're done."

Picking two crayons of different colors from a box of crayons requires making choices. Children with ASD have trouble making choices, and choosing among a box of colored crayons can be cognitively taxing for them. Making choices is the first step to more efficient problem-solving. This is explained in more detail below.

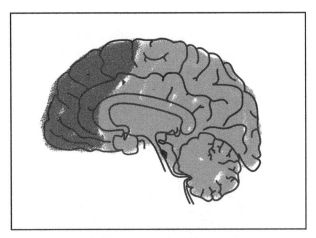

Figure 7.2 Colored brain

Making Choices: Comparing and Contrasting

Making a choice is an example of *comparing and contrasting* as a problem-solving task that requires executive functioning. Thinking about two separate ideas requires using language to compare and contrast two ideas. This makes what would seem a simple choice, choosing among crayons to color parts of the brain, become work. Rather than choosing a crayon, the child will sometimes sit silently as if waiting for a cue or prompt to do something.

Faced with the cognitive task of making a choice, the child will often respond, "I don't care; you choose." This has often been an effective response strategy because (1) it has been a socially appropriate response that does not get the child in trouble; and (2) it allows the child to avoid the cognitively taxing task of actually having to make a choice. When a child keeps repeating the same response ("You chose," or "I don't know what to pick") this is a red flag for me that I will have to help make choices become easier for this child. I explain to the child,

> "Sometimes our brain goes to sleep on us. [I will pretend to snore]. That's what our brain looks like when it goes to sleep on us. When we say, 'I don't know,' or 'I can't do it,' or 'This is too hard,' or 'I don't care—you pick.' This is our brain trying to go to sleep on us."

If I see signs that the child is becoming emotionally dysregulated (rocking, closing her/her eyes, etc.), I say,

> "Your brain is trying to hurt you."

I then tell the child,

> "Your brain is really trying to hurt you by telling you that you are not smart enough to know how to [whatever I had wanted the child to do when he started showing signs of dysregulation]."

Then I tell the child that I need to talk to his brain for a moment, and I start talking directly to the top of his head, saying,

> "Billy's brain; knock it off! Billy is too smart to let you hurt him like this. Billy knows how to guess what to do; he knows how to ask for help."

Then, in a quiet tone, speaking now to the face of the child, not the top of his head, I say,

> "Let me know when you are ready."

Then I wait silently and patiently. This is important; the child needs to know that he needs to tell me when he is ready. A child with ASD often becomes prompt-dependent as independent activation of his frontal lobe is limited or inefficient. He needs to know (and sometimes I explicitly tell the child) that he needs to talk to his brain, just like I did.

If the child again starts to fidget or turn away (again, early signs of emotional dysregulation), I add,

> "I'm confused. Your two choices are either give an answer or ask for help."

Again, I wait for any response, and then praise it. If the child is still reluctant, I may model what to say: "Miss Janice, I need help." When the child repeats it, I then profusely thank the child, and include what he did or said when I praise: "Thank you so much for asking for help. I didn't know what you wanted, but now I do." Even if all the child can do is whisper "Help," I accept. For example, I say,

> "Thank you for asking for help. Now I can help you."

And I then explicitly explain why he needs to ask for help:

> "If I were to help you when you don't ask for help, then I would be treating you like you are not smart."

Then I ask,

> "Are you smart?"

If the child is not able to answer, due to the beginning of emotional dysregulation, I again provide a model:

> "Yes, You are! And it is because you are smart that I need to wait for you to ask for help. Only smart people ask for help."

Here, as in all my sessions, I am constantly explaining why I need the child to verbally express himself. For example, in this case, the *why* is because, "Only smart people ask for help."

I am continuously reminding the child from this moment forward, in every session with the child, that the child is in control of his brain. This is the beginning of independent problem-solving.

Asking for Help

When I see signs of dysregulation in response to a question or activity (e.g. making a choice), whether silence, or verbal or physical actions, then I immediately ask the child,

"Do you need help?"

Whatever verbal response he makes, I accept as a valid request for help. For example, if the child yells, "*Help!*" (a not uncommon response because they quickly become stressed when faced with a challenging situation or activity), I respond in a neutral voice,

"Thank you for asking, I would love to help you."

And then I provide the needed support or scaffolding.

Assessing Whether the Child Understands What a Problem "Feels" Like

The above series of interactions with a therapist will be new for the child, and as something new, it is generally stressful for children with ASD. As was discussed in Chapter 6 ("Step 1: Recognizing that one is in a problem-solving situation"), stress is initially manifested viscerally, as a tightening sensation in the stomach. Children in general, but especially children with ASD, are not consciously aware that they are cognitively stressed, nor do they have a verbal label for "stress." They may not be aware of the visceral experience in their stomach, or if they do, they do not have a label for what the feeling is. Similarly, *stimming* is a sign of emotional excitement, sometimes positive and sometimes negative. When faced with a problem where they don't know how to respond, stimming is the child's subconscious attempt to remain emotionally regulated.

When I ask the child to make a choice, I look for any movement or sound that I hadn't seen before the activity began.

- Did he show movement away from me?
- Did he grunt or make some other verbal response?
- Did he yawn or stretch?

These are signals that the child is beginning to feel stressed. As a therapist I look for these as teaching moments. I point out what the child did to begin helping him understand what a problem feels like. Equally importantly, I give the child *labels* that help the child put words to what he is feeling.

"This is what 'hard' feels like.

This is what 'learning' feels like.

When I see you do...[and I imitate what he just did, e.g. move, grunt, groan, yawn, etc.], this is really your brain telling you it needs help. Everyone's brain is different. My brain makes me yell and cry. Your brain makes you [grunt, etc.]. When your brain does this, it is begging you to ask for help."

Labeling is a language skill. Having a label allows the child to use language to think about what is going on; it is the process of "thinking in speech." In this way, language—that is, labeling—provides the child with a strategy to start understanding what he is viscerally feeling. This then allows the child to interpret the feeling: "What I am feeling is called 'stressed.' When I feel stressed, it is time for me to start 'talking to my brain.'"

First Session Overview

As a clinician, this first session has given me a great deal of understanding of the child's readiness to learn and become an independent problem-solver. Through interaction and observation I have a sense of whether the child views herself as a learner (answers questions directly and readily makes choices), or feels helpless in a learning situation (sits silently without responding, or begins to emotionally dysregulate). I have been able to assess informally whether the child understands what a problem "feels like." And I have begun to understand how the child responds when faced with a problem, such as making a choice.

In addition, this first session gives me a better understanding of other developmental skills. For example, showing a child the picture of the brain gives me insights into:

- *Proprioceptive skills* (the sense of where one's body is at any given moment in time): When I say, "Put your hands on your forehead," I look to see where the child places his hands. If he puts his hands on the back of his head or on the chin, it means the child is still working on a sense of where his body is in relation to space and movement.

- *Literacy:* I ask the child, "Write your name on the picture." Has the child internalized that he is a writer (indicated by whether he simply starts writing his name), or does he not feel competent, and feel the need for an adult to write it "the right way"?

Working with Adolescents and Adults

When I work with an older individual, I modify the process. For an adolescent or adult, I will use a more advanced color drawing of the brain and point to parts of the brain. I do *not* make the individual color it in. However, as with a younger child, I will point to the front part of the brain (the frontal lobe), and tell the individual, "This is the part of your brain you use to think." The lesson, however, remains the same: I will help the individual learn to separate his brain from himself.

How I Conduct My Sessions: Be Fluid and Open to Opportunities

My sessions are fluid; I am always listening for opportunities to help the child learn to understand and cope with situations he deems challenging or stressful. For example, if in the middle of a compare and contrast activity, a child starts to yell, "I don't want to do this anymore!" I stop the activity and focus on the dysregulation the child is experiencing. So if "yelling" comes up in the middle of a compare and contrast activity, I will stop the activity, and focus on the "yelling" situation because it is an opportunity to work on emotional state vocabulary and coping skills. It is what is happening to the child *right now*; it is a learning-moment opportunity.

It is also part of the collaboration I am developing with the child. He and I are collaborating in our session about what it is important to talk about. Moreover, it is often an opportunity to bring the parent into our collaboration. Sometimes the parent will email me ahead of time about something. In other words, our sessions are about problem-solving and independent thinking, not a specific lesson or topic that I want to focus on.

This flexibility is critical to our success. We are developing a long-term relationship; I'm going to be working with the child weekly for months and typically for years. I don't need to follow a specific agenda.

Summary

In this first session I have begun the process of building trust between the child and me. For example, I have made the child feel safe in my room by allowing him to yell or say whatever he needs to say when feeling stressed. The child understands that I will never take anything personally. I have introduced myself as a "brain teacher," and someone that will help him become the boss of his brain. And though I have the expectation that the child will make a choice, something that I know will be cognitively taxing to the child, I have supported whatever choice was made. In so doing, I have encouraged the child to take control of the decision-making process.

In doing all this I have also begun the process of building his self-esteem and self-confidence. I have explained that I will help him become the "boss of his brain." I am beginning the process of showing the child that he can make his own choices rather than rely on others to do so for the child. And I have begun to help the child understand, by providing him with labels, how a visceral feeling is something he can begin to be in control of by using language to talk themselves through it.

Talking to their brain is a problem-solving strategy. Over time, the child will independently begin to talk to his brain. Parents have told me that they have overheard their child literally speaking out loud: "Brain, I need you to wake up." These are words the child has learned in our therapy sessions. This out-loud self-talk will eventually become internalized as true inner speech and the process of *thinking in speech* has begun.

CHAPTER 8

Developing Mental State and Emotions Vocabulary

Expressing negative emotions and feelings is often stressful for a child with autism. Adults working with a child with autism will need to learn to observe the child's body and facial signals for signs of stress or emotional overload, as the child's behavior typically will not match her emotional state. For example, an adult could mistakenly interpret a child's lack of physical affect as a sign of indifference or being oppositional. Minimal or mismatched physical affect and emotion is common in individuals with ASD; understanding and using verbal and nonverbal (i.e. body) language appropriately requires a well-developed theory of mind. When faced with a challenging or stressful activity (typically anything that requires higher-level language), the adult will need to provide support by demonstrating how she felt when faced with stress, and then prompt the child to describe how she feels. The adult will need to provide higher-level language support by writing the vocabulary on a whiteboard (e.g. exasperated, perplexed, frustrated), and then help to discuss her feelings. The child's body tightens, and she will sometimes become fidgety when faced with stress.

As the child is not yet always aware of how a stressful situation is making her body and mental state feel, the child will sometimes appear to deny feeling stressed by a difficult situation. This is an early emerging skill, and an adult will need to describe to the child the physical body movements he sees (e.g. tightening of muscles, fidgety legs) and imitate these for the child, while stating that these are signs her brain is uncomfortable and nervous. The adult needs to state, "Everybody feels stressed when [describe situation] happens, our brain is begging us to ask an adult for help." The adult also needs to let the child know that he (i.e. the adult) felt stressed when he was that age, and this means she is normal.

Intervention

Emotions vocabulary and *mental state vocabulary* are essential for developing self-regulation. We need to be able to think through what it is about the situation that is causing us to be stressed, and reason within our self (using inner speech) to reflect on all that is happening in order to repress our urge to emote in the moment. This requires having the necessary vocabulary to describe what we are feeling or seeing in someone else.

We need *emotions vocabulary* to label how we are feeling: angry, annoyed, frustrated, and so on. These are words typically associated with how we feel *in the moment*, and often have a physical expression associated with them. Contrastingly, mental state vocabulary is typically verbs that reflect thoughts but not actions, for example hope, wish, desire, believe, and so on. These are important for reflecting on what to do, rather than describing an emotion. During my sessions, I work on both interchangeably, depending on what the child is doing or what I want the child to think about during our conversations or activities.

In addition to mental state/emotions vocabulary, we also work on *previously learned knowledge*. Previously learned knowledge is essential for relating what the child is experiencing in a current situation to a similar situation that has occurred to her in the past (comparing and contrasting). Recalling previously learned knowledge reminds the child that what she learned in the past may apply to this new situation.

Developing Emotions Vocabulary

An example of developing emotions vocabulary is understanding the difference between *annoyed* and *aggravated* and *enraged*. These are related emotions but of different levels of intensity. The child needs to develop her emotions vocabulary in order to attach an appropriate label to differing situations.

I start by asking the child a question:

"Tell me a situation where you felt 'annoyed.' [pause] Do you want to go first or do you want me to go first?"

In asking this question, I want to see if the child can retrieve a logical situation for that vocabulary word *on her own*, or whether the child will need help. If the child is not able to answer, I need to look for signs of stress even as the child is silent. When I see any signals of stress during the silence, I model what I want:

> "I was always annoyed when my mother spent more time with my brother than with me."

or

> "I always felt annoyed when my mom told me to clean my room."

or

> "I was annoyed when my brother took my favorite pencil."

Then I ask the child,

> "What was something that happened to you that made you feel annoyed?"

I then wait silently for the child to respond. The child might give me an example that is the right emotion, but is the wrong intensity, such as when the child was enraged. If so I draw the emotion scale (Figure 8.1), and point out where *enraged* falls on the scale (9), versus where *annoyed* falls on the scale (3). Then I state,

> "That sounds like you were "enraged"; that's like a 9 on the scale.

Then I give an example of when I was enraged.

Figure 8.1 Hand-drawn emotions scale

Alternatively, the child might give me an example of a situation that is the right intensity, but the wrong emotion (e.g. feeling afraid). When this happens, I respond,

> "That's great trying, but it's not quite annoyed."

I ask the child for a different situation that was annoying, and if she still doesn't give a correct (or reasonable) response, I watch her actions to see how she is feeling, and I might say,

"You look like you're annoyed at me right now. Are you feeling annoyed at me right now?"

Then I wait for the child to verbally tell me that she is feeling annoyed at me. Typically children will not want to respond in the affirmative, because they are confused: I'm asking if I am creating a negative emotion, but they're afraid to tell me that this is what I'm doing.

When I see the child seems reluctant to respond, I ask again and nod my head in the affirmative. I might have to model the statement the child should make. For example, while nodding my head, I say,

"Miss Janice, you're making me feel annoyed."

Then I help the child say this on her own.

Whether it is the situation I just created, or if the child comes up with her own reasonable example of "annoyed," I then help her generalize it. I immediately say,

"You know what—everyone feels annoyed when that happens to them. Mom feels annoyed when that happens to her; your sister feels annoyed when that happens to her; other students feel annoyed; your friends feel annoyed. Everyone feels annoyed sometimes."

Every time I tell children that *everyone* gets annoyed, they are surprised. They don't know this; they typically think they are the only ones who have felt this way. I then explain,

"The reason you don't know this is that they are using self-talk; they are saying to their brain, 'she is making me annoyed,' but you can't hear it."

I then give an explicit example of self-talk, that is, saying out loud what I am saying to my brain silently.

"'My mom can be so annoying when she stops me from playing my game.' But I don't say it out loud. I say it to my brain. When you have these thoughts, you're not being bad; you're being normal. *Everyone*, even Mom (and I point to Mom if she is in the room), sometimes says this to themselves. *But* we don't say it out loud; we tell it silently to our brain. Every boy and girl on the planet thinks that sometimes their parents are annoying. It is normal to be annoyed sometimes."

This is helping the child understand that being normal doesn't mean being perfect. I go on to explain:

> "When we let our brain hurt us by pretending we're perfect and are never annoyed, our brain 'EXPLODES.' When my brain explodes it makes me scream or yell or cry."

I want them to acknowledge this, so I ask,

> "What do you when your brain EXPLODES?"

The child might respond by saying, "I cry and sometimes I yell." Then I say,

> "That's because your brain is hurting you by telling you that you need to be perfect. But you know what—*nobody's* perfect. *Everybody* makes mistakes.
>
> The trick is to make different mistakes, because we're always going to make mistakes.
>
> I've already made three mistakes this morning. How many mistakes do you think I've made since you came here?"

Then we might talk about the mistakes I made. Now we're talking about feelings and mistakes and how that's normal, and the child is able to do this calmly. Then I explain,

> "That's why I'm going to annoy your brain on purpose. I'm going to hurt your brain on purpose, because I want your brain to start listening to *you*, so you can make it stop hurting you!
>
> I wish our brains learned differently; but this will help you practice telling your brain to stop hurting you.
>
> This is *hard work*. But that's what learning feels like; it's *hard work*. But you can do hard work because you are *smart!*"

During these interactions I look for signs of stress. When I see them, I stop the activity, and model the behavior and state, for example,

> "Cheryl, you're showing me you are feeling stressed."

I intentionally use the words "feeling" as well as "stressed." I want Cheryl to start recognizing what feeling stressed looks like and feels like so she will recognize it on her own.

"Cheryl, when you tighten your muscles and squeeze your hand into your legs like this, your brain is telling me that it is stuck and you need to ask for help.

When I hear, 'Miss Janice, can you help me?' I can help you."

We then, as needed, digress into "asking for help" instruction.

At the end of the session, I ask the child, "How many times did I annoy your brain today?" If the child answers "three," I might respond, "Oh, I thought it was four or five." Some children (typically it's a boy) tell me "ten"! Then I might respond, "Wow, I really annoyed your brain today!"[1] What they say is not important. I do this because I want them to be analyzing and thinking about this before they leave.

Emotions Vocabulary and Multiple Solutions: "It's Not the End of the World!"

Part of developing true problem-solving skills, in contrast to teaching stimulus–response dyads, is being able to generate multiple solutions to a problem, and then making a choice. I sometimes combine this with developing emotional state vocabulary.

"Cheryl, imagine after you got dressed for school, you spilled juice on your blouse at breakfast. Give me a 'happy' solution and an 'unhappy' solution. What would a 'happy' solution be?"

I always ask for the "happy" solution first. Thinking about a "happy" solution is less likely to cause as much dysregulation, and I want the child to be able to pause, reflect and generate a solution with as little stress-causing effort as possible.

Depending on the amount of prompting the child needs, we work on a positive (happy) solution. For example, eventually the child tells me,

Cheryl: "I could change into a clean blouse."

Janice: "Right, you could change into a clean blouse. That's a happy solution."

---

1 For as many years as I have been doing this, no child has ever asked me in return how many times they annoyed me.

Then I prompt an unhappy solution:

> Janice: "What would happen if you *didn't* have time to change into a clean blouse?"

> Cheryl: "I would have to go to school with juice on my blouse."

At this point, the child will start to show signs of dysregulation. I quickly add,

> Janice: "Is it the end of the world if you go to school with juice on your blouse?"

> Cheryl: "No."

> Janice: "Right, it is *not* the end of the world. Why is it not 'the end of the world'?"

Then, because this is a stressful question, I quickly prompt her to think about why it is not "the end of the world."

> "Do you still get to come home after school? ['Yes.']

> Do Mom and Dad still love you? ['Yes.']

> Do you still get to go to school tomorrow? ['Yes.']

> Do you get to wear a clean blouse to school tomorrow? ['Yes.']

> Right. But how would you *feel?* ['Embarrassed.']

> Yes. I would feel embarrassed too, if I came to work with a stain on my blouse. Mom would feel embarrassed. Dad would feel embarrassed if he went to work with juice on his shirt.

> Everyone feels embarrassed when they have to go to school or work with something on their blouse.

> BUT…it's *not* the end of the world."

This is helping Cheryl develop theory of mind: she would feel embarrassed; other people would feel embarrassed just like her. But feeling embarrassed is not the end of the world; it's just feeling embarrassed like everyone else.

As the child realizes this, I see her physically relax, and sometimes giggle because she knows it's not the end of the world.

Prompting Negative Emotions to Develop Coping and Problem-Solving

When working with a child with ASD, an extremely important component of the intervention is to help the child understand her negative emotions, that is, emotions that feel uncomfortable, such as feeling ignored, lonely, embarrassed, and so on. Each week I might work on a different emotional word. For example, I might ask the child to tell me a situation where she felt *mad*.

Bobby: "Yesterday. Mom yelled at me when I was on the computer."

Janice: "Wait a minute, I'm confused. Did Mom just start yelling at you *for no reason?!?*"

It is critical to add "for no reason." I am setting a foundation for cause-and-effect problem-solving. Adding "for no reason" requires the child to pause, reflect, and think about what was going on, not just recall the emotion.

Bobby: "No."

Janice: "What happened? What were you doing?"

Bobby: "I was playing computer games."

Janice: "Was Mom yelling at you because you were playing computer games?"

Bobby: "I don't know."

Janice: "Bobby, Mom *never* allows you to play computer games?"

Bobby: "*Yes*, I'm allowed to play computer games."

Janice: "Wait a minute, I'm confused. Did Mom just start yelling at you *for no reason?!?*"

Bobby: "No."

Janice: "I wonder what happened *before* you started playing computer games?"

Bobby: "I was supposed to do my homework."

Janice: "What happened? Why did you choose to have Mom yell at you?"

Bobby: "I didn't choose to have Mom yell at me!!!"

I then begin an "on the one hand, on the other hand" gesture.

> Janice: "Okay. Help me out; I'm confused. It sounds like you had two choices. [I put out one hand as if to put something on it] Do your homework to show Mom how smart you are so you can then play on the computer, or [I put out the other hand as if to put something on it] Don't do your homework and play on the computer, and have Mom yell at you.

In this exchange, I am leading Bobby down a path that leads to understanding that he made a choice a rule. He chose to not do his homework and instead play on the computer, and have Mom yell at him, rather than to do his homework to show Mom how smart he is, and then to play on the computer.

He and I work on how he can help himself think through choice-making and cause–effect relations, so that he is able to tell himself, "I chose to have Mom get mad at me." Over time, Bobby learns to think through situations, which then allows him to make better choices. He demonstrates this during the chit-chat part of subsequent sessions by talking about new situations, where "I forgot to talk to my brain when I…[lied to my mother about xxx]," or when he tells me, "I chose to show Mom how smart I am by…"

This process describes how he is developing inner speech. First, he and I discuss this with me asking questions until he verbalizes what he should be telling himself in that situation. Later, for example at home, he might talk to himself or whisper to himself about the choice he needs to make (private speech). Eventually, he thinks about this choice in his head to himself, using inner speech to problem-solve.

Learning Who Are Friends and Who Are Bullies

I use this same interactive process to help a child learn who are real friends and who are bullies. It is not uncommon that when I ask a child to tell me when she was upset or had their feelings hurt, I hear about a time when she was bullied.

> Suzy: "Cindy wouldn't play with me. She lied to me and then she hit me."

Janice: "Suzy, I'm confused. Why do you want to hang out with someone who lies to you and hits you?"

Suzy: "Because sometimes she is nice."

Janice: "So that's your *choice*. You choose to hang out with her. What *else* could you do?"

This is helping her think through a social problem. First, I'm helping her realize this is a *choice*; she has control over the situation. Second, I'm prompting her to think about other options (choices) she could make.

Janice: "What *else* could you do?"

Suzy: [Silence] or "I don't know."

Janice: "Could you find other friends who don't lie to you or hit you?"

Suzy: "Yes."

Janice: "Who else is in your class that you could hang out with who doesn't lie or hit you?"

This is social problem-solving; it involves choice-making, comparing and contrasting, pulling up previously learned knowledge about other peers who she has been with in similar situations, and so on. More importantly, it is problem-solving she can use to help herself stay safe. It is well recognized in the literature that children with ASD are at a higher risk for being rejected by their peers or bullied. Teaching a child to independently problem-solve allows the child to recognize peers who are not bullies and who is safe to develop friendships with.

CHAPTER 9

Vocabulary Development for Higher-Level Use of Language for Problem-Solving

Vocabulary development is more than mere labeling or naming a person or object. Vocabulary development requires efficient executive functioning. It requires a deep understanding of how these words facilitate retention and retrieval of previously learned knowledge, and access this knowledge for reasoning and problem-solving. For example, the word "cow" represents more than simply a picture of a cow. In our mind, "cow" is understood in relationship to other animals: that is, where we find cows, what they do for us, and so on. Depending on the context of what we are reading or what the question is, our concept of a cow involves:

- what animal group it belongs in
- the parts of a cow
- where we typically find cows
- why cows are important to us.

This complex representation of a cow is referred to a robust vocabulary; it is a deeper understanding of the relationship of "cow" to us and to everything else. Developing robust vocabulary is essential when using language for higher-order problem-solving,

Robust Vocabulary Development for Early Learners

Initially, I help Billy develop a simple cognitive category, for example, *farm animals*. I show Billy a picture of a cow, and ask,

> "What kind of animal is this?" [Billy is able to provide the appropriate label: "cow."]

If he is speaking in complete sentences, my expectation is that he responds in complete sentences. I prompt as follows:

> "It's…" [pause]. If no response, then "It's a…" [pause].

We do this until he gives me the full response, "It is a cow." Then I take out my dry erase board and write the word "cow" at the top (Figure 9.1).

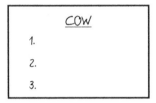

Figure 9.1 Teaching simple category development ("Cow")

> "What kind of animal is it?"

The answer I want is, "A cow is a farm animal." I prompt Billy to say both the full sentence and the category, "farm animal." Then I write on the first line, "farm animal." Note that I want him to say the complete sentence ("A cow is a farm animal."), but I only write "farm animal" on the whiteboard (Figure 9.2).

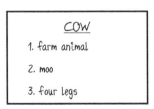

Figure 9.2 Showing characteristics for the "Cow" category

Then I ask him, "What else can you tell me about a cow?" Each time I require that he use complete sentence: "A cow says moo." "A cow has four legs." Then he and I do the same thing for another picture. This starts the process of developing simple cognitive categories.

Complex Category Development

Once Billy is able to provide simple categories, I can start helping Billy develop more complex categorization processes that require true problem-solving. This time I take out two whiteboards. On the first, I write at the top "COW—Dog—BOTH" as shown in Figure 9.3. Then I ask,

"How are cows and dogs alike?"

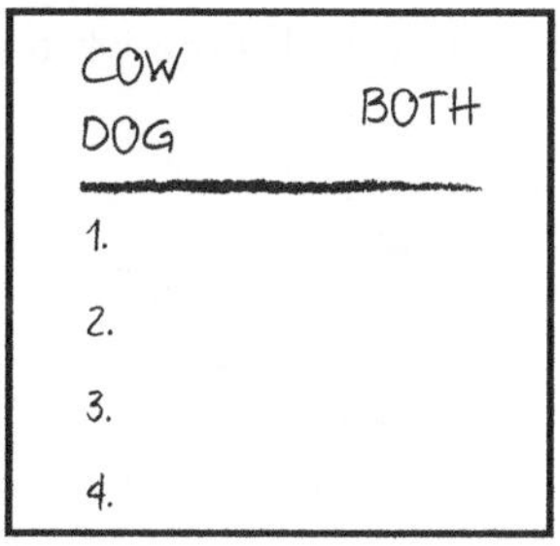

Figure 9.3 Setting up the dry erase board for
comparing animals with *similar* attributes
(How "Cow" and "Dog" are the same)

This kind of compare-and-contrast question is often challenging for children with ASD. Their brains naturally hold items in separate, distinct categories—that is, one item per category. This is why labeling individual items tends to be easy for children on the spectrum. In contrast, recognizing similarities is a difficult compare-and-contrast cognitive task. Comparing and contrasting requires holding onto and mentally manipulating multiple pieces of information to solve the same problem. This process is part of executive functioning.

In the beginning I help Billy with prompts:

"Cows and dogs are both…" [pause]

Then I wait for a correct answer. Usually, the first response is "animals." While correct, I want Billy to start thinking at a deeper level about the similarities of two seemingly very different types of animals. I acknowledge "animals" in order to maintain Billy's emotional regulation and because I want Billy to keep looking and thinking:

"Well, you're right; they're both animals."

Then directing his attention to the pictures, I ask,

"How are they the same?"

I again help Billy formulate a complete sentence: "Cows and dogs are both animals," and then write his response on the whiteboard. Then I ask again,

"How else are they the same?"

We do this several times, until we fill the whiteboard (Figure 9.4).

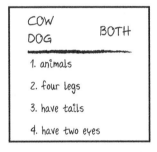

Figure 9.4 Comparing animals with *similar* attributes

Then I ask Billy to tell me how they're different. Differences are easier for a child to describe, because the differences are more salient or more noticeable. I pick up the second whiteboard and make two columns with the word "BUT" in the middle (see Figure 9.5). The "BUT" will be important to help him form "difference" sentences.

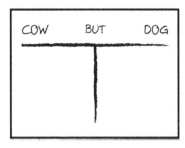

Figure 9.5 Setting up the dry erase board for
contrasting animals with *different* attributes

"What kind of animal is a cow?"

If Billy says, "A cow is a farm animal," I enthusiastically say, "That's right!" If he just says "farm animal," I prompt him, "A cow is…[pause], and wait until he tells me the full sentence ("A cow is a farm animal."). Then, "What kind of animal is a dog?" Repeating the process, we get to "A dog is a pet." Then,

"So, how are a cow and a dog different?"

We then work on saying the complete compound sentence, "A cow is a farm animal, *but* a dog is a pet." Including and requiring "but" in the middle of the compound sentence ensures that Billy will pause and reflect (take a moment to think) about what he knows about cows and what he knows about dogs (recalling previously learned knowledge). This is also cognitively challenging because it requires him to keep in mind two separate pieces of information at the same time, and determine how a dog and cow are similar to each other and how they are different from each other (compare and contrast).

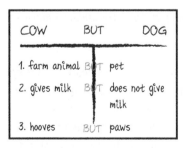

Figure 9.6 Contrasting animals with *different* attributes

I then ask Billy to give me another example of how cows and dogs are different. Since this is effortful for Billy, I watch for signs of either physical dysregulation or a precursor of dysregulation, *guessing*. Guessing often occurs as a problem-solving strategy intended to reduce stress—getting me to stop asking questions that tax his brain, rather than pausing and reflecting, pulling up previously learned knowledge, and so on. When I hear guessing or see signs of dysregulation, I quickly interject, "Do you need help?" Then I wait for him to tell me, "Miss Janice, I need help," and then I help him.

These activities also offer opportunities for a child to learn new vocabulary or concepts, in addition to retrieving previously learned knowledge. For example, when looking for differences in pictures of dogs and cows a child might say, "Cows and dogs have different feet." At that point, I explain,

> "We don't say cows have feet; we say cows have [pause] 'hooves.' What do we call [point to 'foot'] of a dog? [Child responds, 'paws.'] That's right! A dog has [paws]. What other animal has paws? [Child: 'a cat.'] That's right; cats and dogs both have paws. And they're both pets!"

A lot is going on in the interaction above. I am helping Billy begin to develop a mental framework for cognitive categorization (how things are the same and how things are different), which is essential for problem-solving. For him to do this, he must use many elements of the *Thinking in Speech* model of problem-solving:

- He's being required to pull up *previously learned knowledge.*
- He is having to *pause and reflect.*
- He is *making choices.*
- He is *developing in-depth vocabulary knowledge.*
- He is *asking for help.*

Sometimes these interactions can lead in unexpected directions. As an example, a child and I were talking about the differences between cows and dogs. When I asked if dogs give milk, the child responded, "Well, technically they do?" I used this to work on his thinking about language, and in particular, a deeper understanding of word meaning. In English, one can infer from the sentences "A cow gives milk," and

"A goat gives milk," that the two animals are used for supplying milk to people. The sentences "A dog gives milk," and "A hamster gives milk," sound odd because they imply that we use these animals to supply us with milk, which our previously learned knowledge tells us they do not. I responded,

"Yes, technically[1] they do, but 'giving milk' has a special meaning."

Then before he responded, I stated,

"Do we get milk from dogs?"

My tone is important when asking these questions. I am not trying to correct the child, rather I am helping him to think about a deeper, more abstract meaning of "giving milk": giving milk is something we associate with cows, and not with dogs.

A category framework provides the child with the ability to manipulate new information in similar and different contexts: that is, to think about information, rather than just collect and remember new information without a meaningful conceptual understanding. Without a category schema to process new information or experiences, each new experience is processed as a discrete incident. Deeper understanding of vocabulary is critical before thinking about ourselves and others can begin.

---

1 When the child gave me this response, he was not actually being technical; he was being specific. He recalled a discrete piece of information, rather than thinking about the deeper meanings of the words and sentence structure.

CHAPTER 10

Answering Questions Logically

Children with ASD have difficulty answering questions logically. Answering a question is an example of a dialogic interaction. An example of a monologic interaction would be to simply talk about what one knows (i.e. a monologue). Dialogic interactions are much more complex, in that they require individuals to understand questions posed to them, understand *how* to answer the question, retrieve world knowledge about the content of the question, know that sometimes they will have to pause and listen to someone else, and formulate a verbal response. This requires effortful and sustained brain activation and cognitive processing that neurotypical individuals do naturally, without formal instruction.

The above-mentioned multifaceted effort can be stressful, and cause emotional dysregulation. This is why children with ASD often stim when asked a question; as noted previously, stimming reflects the child's effort to maintain emotional self-control. Thus answering a logical question requires both cognitive effort towards accomplishing the task—answering the question—and remaining emotionally regulated.

The focus of this chapter is helping children with ASD learn *how* to answer questions. Children with ASD need to be explicitly taught that the wording of a question is a cue for what kind of answer is appropriate. It can never be assumed that the child isn't answering the question due to lack of comprehension, but first and foremost, one must look at the child's understanding of the grammatical and sentence structure necessary for answering various questions. For example, if I hold up a plastic toy dog, and ask a child, "Is this a banana?" I can never assume that the child does not know the difference between a dog and a banana. I must first informally assess if a child typically only answers yes to all yes/no questions, and then whether the child merely labels the object when shown it (i.e. says "dog" when shown a plastic toy dog) or answers, "No, that is not a banana." I explain below how to help children consistently and independently answer yes/no questions if they are not yet doing so.

Answering Yes/No Questions: Teaching "Yes"

In my office I have a big bucket of common objects. For this activity I reach into the bucket and pull out one of the objects, for example a plastic dog.

I point to the object, and ask,

"Is this a dog?"

Bobby labeled objects instead of answering yes, and was not yet able to respond to "no" questions. For example, when asked, "Is this a dog?" Bobby responded with the label "dog," and not "Yes, this is a dog." In doing so, Bobby had *not* answered the question; answering the question properly requires a yes/no response. Instead, Bobby *labeled* the object. Labeling is a simpler cognitive process than answering a yes/no question. Labeling only requires that Bobby access his world knowledge about what a dog looks like, and verbalize the label. Answering a yes/no question requires extra cognitive steps. He has to compare and contrast the object to the category, and then respond appropriately to the question with a "Yes" or a "No."

When I hear a child respond with a label, I need to explicitly state why that was not the correct answer. For example:

"I didn't ask *what* this was, I asked a 'yes/no' question."

Often I have to model the right way to answer,

"Yes, that is a dog."

It should be noted at this point that I am not going to require a complete sentence, *but* I do need to hear a "yes," as this is the correct response to a "yes" question.

I then ask Bobby to repeat the answer or just the word "yes" that I modeled. If he again responds "dog," I again model the correct response. If Bobby looks like he isn't sure what to do, I use the strategy known as phonemic cueing, or stating the first sound or two of the word to facilitate word retrieval: "Y…" or "Ye…." To reiterate, in the initial stages of this activity, I am less concerned with a complete answer than I am that he understands that a yes/no question requires an answer of "Yes" or "No."

When Bobby eventually gives a "yes" answer, I explicitly praise the "yes" answer, and tell him to toss the object into another bucket. (That was the fun part for Bobby.) Then I pick another object from the bucket, and repeat the same process. We repeat this several times until I see he's getting tired of it and starting to become fidgety or dysregulated. I continue this in our next session as necessary, until Bobby consistently responds with the appropriate "yes" response.

Once Bobby has mastered answering, "Yes," I can start helping him learn how to answer "No" questions.

Answering Yes/No Questions: Teaching "No"

Answering "No" to a yes/no question is more difficult than answering "Yes." Both answers require accessing world knowledge. However, the executive functioning to reach a logical conclusion is different. A "yes" response is more straightforward; the child searches her memory (*previously learned knowledge*) until she finds the matching vocabulary word, and then must verbalize "Yes." To answer "No" the child reaches a conclusion based on comparing and contrasting multiple vocabulary words and then coming up with the logical conclusion of "No, that is not a…"As with teaching "yes," I pull an object from the bucket, for example a cat, and then ask an absurd question:

"Is this Mommy?" (Mom is in the room with me during therapy.)

This question requires the child to compare and contrast "cat" with "Mommy" and then respond "No." Initially, the child is confused as no one has ever asked her this question before. I then repeat the question with more facial and vocal expression. I point to Mommy, while looking at the cat, and with an exaggerated voice and expression, ask,

"Is *this* Mommy?"

I might shake my head to encourage the child to say, "No." If the child responds "Cat," a labeling response, I tell the child,

"Wait. This is not a 'What is it' question; this is a 'yes/noooo' question" [emphasizing the word "no."]

I repeat the question, if necessary pointing to Mom while looking at the object, possibly even using phonemic cueing, "N...," until she eventually says, "No." I then respond enthusiastically, "That's right! No, not Mommy."

I have the child toss the object in the bucket, then I take out another object, and repeat the process with the next object, again asking the question, "Is this Mommy?"

Once the child can consistently answer, "No, that's not Mommy," I switch to more difficult, less absurd questions, for example, when shown a pig, I ask "Is this a horse?" When the child is able to consistently answer "no" questions, I start mixing up "yes" and "no" questions.

The above activities are intended to help the child learn how to answer yes/no questions. When a child uses a label to answer a yes/no question, she is attending only to the object. My goal is to get her to pay attention to the wording (logic) of the question, as well as the object, and compare and contrast it with her previously learned knowledge. Over time, I switch from three-dimensional objects to two-dimensional pictures. When working with older children, I use pictures (two-dimensional) instead of objects (three-dimensional) from the start of the activity.

Answering Questions Logically

Once a child with ASD understands *how* to answer basic yes/no questions, I can move on to logically answering other kinds of questions. For example,

"Do we eat rocks?"

"Is sugar sweet?"

"Is a pillow soft?"

"Do we eat dirt?"

Answering all of these questions requires world knowledge, but more importantly it requires knowing that answering a question is not labeling, but recognizing key words in the question as a cue for how to answer a question. Once the child understands that the words in a question determine how to answer the question, I can move on to more challenging wh- questions.

Answering *Wh-* Questions: Sally
What Questions

The first *wh-* questions I start with are *what* questions. *What* questions are the easiest *wh-* questions, because they are, essentially, labeling questions. As with yes/no questions, my goal is to help Sally learn how to answer *what* questions: that is, the structure of the response she needs to use to appropriately answer a *what* question.

I use commonly used commercial "*what*" cards for teaching *what* questions. I start by telling Sally what we will be doing:

"We're going to work on *what* questions."

I then take two to four cards from the deck in front of her, each showing a different object. The number of cards depends on the child's scanning ability. As an example, if one of the cards is an umbrella, I then ask,

"*What* do you use when it rains?"

In this case, from my past experience with Sally, I know that she has sufficient verbal ability to answer with a complete sentence. But she hasn't been explicitly taught to give complete sentences in response to a *what* question. My goal is for Sally to give me a complete-sentence answer: "You use an umbrella when it rains."

Like many children with ASD, Sally will just stare at the cards, or at me, or she may point to the card with the umbrella, but not say anything. If she stares at me or the cards, I ask again. I may need to look at the cards as a cue to Sally that the answer is in front of her. I may need to do other cuing to help her focus on the correct card. Sometimes I may physically help her use her finger to drag the correct card away from the others to make it more salient for her.

Then I repeat the question. Because Sally has sufficient verbal ability, I model the full answer:

"You use an umbrella when it rains."

When she eventually responds with a full statement, I then explicitly praise what she did so as to help her learn how to answer *what* questions with complete responses.

"That's right; you use an umbrella when it rains. You just answered a *what* question. *What* do you use when it rains? You use an umbrella."

Then we move on to another card, and repeat the same process. As always, my goal is helping her know *how* to respond to a *what* question. In the very beginning, the emphasis is on helping her learn the vocabulary and sentence structure for answering these types of questions, not treating it as a test question. In other words, she is learning to use the words in the question as a cue for helping her provide a complete answer. I do this with Sally until I see that she is getting tired, or feeling overwhelmed.

When she is getting fidgety or frustrated, I tell her what to expect before we can stop.

"We need to do two [or one, depending on how dysregulated she has become] more, and then you can take a break."

This allows Sally to be able to predict what to expect, which allows her to focus better, and allows her to complete the activity successfully.

We repeat this activity over numerous sessions, until she is able to respond in full sentences consistently. There is no set time frame for how many sessions this will take. For some children it may take three or four sessions; for others we may spend months on this.

Where Questions

To help Sally learn to answer *where* questions, I use "*where*" question cards. This time I explain that we are going to work on *where* questions. I place a card in front of her, such as a picture of an umbrella, and ask her,

"*Where* do you use an umbrella?"

If Sally answers, "rain," I respond,

"That's a great answer to a *when* question (i.e. When do we use an umbrella? We use an umbrella when it rains); I want a *where* answer."

I want Sally to say "Outside." If she cannot come up with an answer on her own, I help her:

"Do you use an umbrella in the house?"

When Sally says, "No," or shakes her head, I respond,

> "That's right, we don't use an umbrella *in* the house. *Where* do we use an umbrella?"

If she still can't answer the question, I give a different cue:

> "Do we use an umbrella in the car?"

Again, when Sally says, "No," or shakes her head, I respond,

> "That's right, we don't use an umbrella in the car. *Where* do we use an umbrella?"

Eventually, Sally will say, often with a questioning tone, "Outside." As this shows Sally is understanding the concept of *where*, I respond,

> "That's right; we use an umbrella outside. Outside is *where* we use an umbrella. You've answered a *where* question. So…*where* do we use an umbrella?"

This time, I want her to give me a full sentence. I may need to help her, so I use phonemic cueing or state the first two to three words of the sentence, until she says the full sentence,

> "W…
>
> We…
>
> We use…
>
> We use an umb…"

And when Sally eventually says the full sentence, I respond,

> "That's right; we use an umbrella outside. You know how to answer a *where* question. Let's try a different one."

I take out a different card, for example a picture of a child sleeping, and ask another *where* question:

> "Where do you go to sleep?"

We repeat the same process. She may at first answer, "Bed." I work with her to answer with a full sentence, "We sleep in a bed." As with *what* questions, we do this until Sally can consistently answer the *where* questions with a full sentence.

When Questions

I teach how to answer *when* questions the same way, again starting with "*when*" cards. This time I explain that we are going to answer *when* questions. I place a card in front of her, such as the picture of an umbrella, and ask her,

"*When* do you use an umbrella?"

The answer I want is, "When it rains." As with other *wh-* questions, one-word answers are a start, but my goal will be a complete sentence. I use the same modeling process to help Sally give a full answer: "We use an umbrella when it rains." We continue with the *when* questions until she is able to consistently give a complete sentence.

As Sally is learning to answer *wh-* questions, she is also learning grammar and sentence structure, specifically how answers are the inverse structure to a question:

When do we use an umbrella?

We use an umbrella *when* it rains.

Learning how to answer these *wh-* questions, as well as learning that a correct answer is structured by using the question, are critical skills, not just for expressive language, but also for reading comprehension. Understanding how to answer these various types of questions also leads to understanding how to answer more abstract *why* questions.

CHAPTER 11

Mental Flexibility to Generate Multiple Solutions

Developing Mental Flexibility

Children with ASD have underdeveloped mental flexibility. That is, they have difficulty shifting thoughts or topics. I see this when I ask them to give me two endings to a story. For example, I say,

> "You spill juice on your blouse when you're getting ready to go to school. Give me two *different* endings to this story, one happy and the other unhappy."

When I ask a question like this, requiring two endings, I have to be explicit and provide the child with two distinct categories, *happy* and *unhappy*. If I just ask for two endings, I do not get two different endings, rather I get an ending and then an extension of the initial ending. For example, Sharon might say for the first ending,

> "I went upstairs and changed my blouse. The end."

And then she might say for the second ending,

> "I went upstairs and changed my blouse. And then I came downstairs. The end."

These are not two different endings; the second is simply an extension of the first. This is an example of mental *in*flexibility. Sharon is unable to shift thoughts or topics. By explicitly asking for two different endings, one happy and one unhappy, I am requiring her to stop the one ending topic she's thought of, and get ready to think about a different ending.

Generating multiple solutions is a difficult executive processing task. It requires multiple components of the problem-solving model:

using previously learned knowledge, choice-making, pausing and reflecting, and using inner speech to think through the situation.

Intervention

I typically use one of two strategies to help a child retrieve previous learned knowledge, depending on the child's problem-solving ability. For example, if the child's problem-solving skills are just emerging, I would likely start with a *forced-choice* strategy. In a problem requiring the child to ask someone for money, for instance, I ask,

"Would you go to your father, or would you go to a neighbor?"

The logical choice would be to go to the father, because this is who the child has gone to in the past (previously learned knowledge). It is also comparing and contrasting. The child must compare each choice (Dad, neighbor) to their previously learned knowledge of who they've asked in the past: "I've asked Dad, but I've never asked my neighbor. Therefore, I will ask Dad."

My other strategy for building problem-solving ability when the child is more advanced, is to give only one response, but one that is clearly absurd or illogical: "Would you go to your neighbor?" This is more challenging because it is not something likely to be part of the child's previously learned knowledge because he has never done this before. There is nothing specific to retrieve; the child must hold this choice in his head while thinking about all past related situations and reach a conclusion that because he has never seen or experienced this, it is not a good choice. Another example of using a totally absurd hypothetical suggestion:

"Would you stand on your roof and say, 'I need money'?"

The child knows this is illogical; he knows this because when he activates his previously learned knowledge, he will not be able to find an example of anyone ever having gone onto a roof and asked for money.

When the child says, "No," I respond,

"You're right. I've never seen anyone stand on the roof and shout, 'I need money'; have you?"

Asking this as a question requires the child to pause and think about why this is not a good answer. The goal is to ensure that the child is actively thinking about *why* it is not a good answer (this is what is known as *meta-cognition* or thinking about thinking).

The next step would be to suggest solutions that may be inappropriate, but not necessarily absurd.

> "Mom has been feeling sad recently. You want to give her something to help her feel better, but you don't have any money. What could you do?"

I wait five to ten seconds, expectantly looking at the child to see if he can come up with a logical solution. If he is unable to respond, I look for initial signs of emotional dysregulation (which is any movement, no matter how slight, that I did not see before). Then I offer a possible solution, not necessarily a logical solution.

> "Could you ask your neighbor for money?"

If the child responds, "Yeah, I could ask my neighbor for money," I shake my head no:

> "That's a great guess, but no, we can't ask a neighbor for money. I wonder what else you could do."

I use my dry erase board and write, "Mom sick, Buy gift, No money," to provide a visual of the important pieces of the problem situation. I then write three choices on another board (Dad, Neighbor, Teacher) and ask the child to pick who would be the best choice for solving this particular problem. I then tell the child, "You have all the answers in front of you. Now tell me in a complete sentence."

Mom sick

Buy gift

No money

Dad

"I would ask Dad for money so I can buy a gift for Mom."

Examples of other possible prompts:

"If you can't go *outside* the house, where else can you go?" [open-ended]

or

"*Inside* the house or *outside* the house?" [forced choice: "Inside."]

(Explicit praise: "Right, inside. I like how you're thinking about this.")

"*Who* in your house could you ask? Could you ask your brother?

Does your brother always want to give you things? ['No.']

Would he give you the money? ['Maybe.']

Right. Maybe. Is he always going to want to give you money? ['No.']

Who else in your house would want to give you money? ['Dad.'] Right, Dad.

Do Dad and Mom talk to each other? ['Yes.']

That's right. So what else would you have to tell Dad?"

More than likely, the child will not be able to tell me what else he has to tell Dad, so after a pause, I model it for him:

"Please don't tell Mom I asked for money."

and then wait for him to repeat it. Then I ask,

"Money for what? ['A gift.'] Right, a gift.

So, what's everything you have to ask Dad?"

I point to the whiteboard that has all of our notes, and then I wait for him to answer, or model the full response.

Mom sick

Buy gift

No money

Dad

"I have to ask Dad for money for a gift for Mom, and I have to ask him not to tell Mom."

I wait for the child to repeat it, and use prompts to help, if necessary.

I had a discussion with Jeremy about asking his neighbor for money. I had to explain the *why* behind the rule that you can't ask a neighbor for money. When I asked who else you could ask for money, Jeremy answered, "My neighbor." I then had to explain the *Never ask your neighbor for money* rule.

Jeremy responded, "Why not?"

"Well, do your parents work hard for their money? ['Yes.'] That's right; your parents work hard for their money.

Do you think your neighbor works hard for their money? ['Yes.'] That's right, they work hard for their money, too.

So, do you think they would be happy if you asked them for money? [and when I say this I shake my head, indicating 'no.' [Jeremy: 'No.']

Do you think your mom would be happy if your neighbor asked your mom for money? ['No.']

What if I asked *you* for money? Would you be happy? ['No.']

So, do you think your neighbor would be a good person to ask for money for your mom's gift? ['No.']

That's right. So that's why we have a rule that says we never ask neighbors or friends for money."

Overview

This entire interaction is an example of developing a single problem-solving *process*, which is more complex than recalling or generating a learned correct response. This sequence is helping the child develop a problem-solving *process* that he can use to put constraints on what might be an overwhelming question: Where can I look; Who can I ask; and so on.

This one situation required several components of the problem-solving model:

- *Using previously learned knowledge:* Where one's money comes from (someone has to work for it); thinking about whether Mom and Dad talk to each other, and so on. Also, knowing the rule for asking for money (i.e. who are we allowed to ask for money), which in this case also meant learning a new rule.

- *Choice-making, and compare and contrast:* Who should I ask, and who should I not ask.

- *Pausing and reflecting:* Taking time to reflect on who would be the best choice to ask, and thinking through other considerations (who does Dad talk to; what else do I need to tell him?) before going to him.

The back-and-forth dialogue that the child and I have serves as a model for him to become an independent problem-solver. My goal is that he will learn to silently think through a problem on his own using the *process* we went through together. My ultimate goal is not for the child to have a dialogue with me about how to help Mom feel better, but for the child to transition to having this dialogue silently with himself: to talk to his brain softly (private speech), and ultimately to have this dialogue in his head—*inner speech*—rather than out loud.

More importantly, my goal is not to teach him what to do when Mom feels bad, but for the child to generalize this complex problem-solving process—pausing and reflecting before responding, using emotional state vocabulary, realizing that how he would feel is how others would feel (theory of mind), using previously learned knowledge to compare and contrast this new situation to situations in the past—in order to generalize his problem-solving ability to similar but different situations that he will experience in the future.

CHAPTER 12

Developing Theory of Mind

Understanding Theory of Mind

Theory of mind (ToM) involves two components, self-insight and other-perspective. Before we can understand what another person is experiencing or thinking, we need to understand ourselves—our own interests, desires, beliefs, strengths, weaknesses, and so on. Once self-insight is in place, then we need to understand that others may have different core values. Thus, in order for *me* to understand why someone else is not interested in what I am interested in, it is first necessary that I understand that what I think is interesting is an interest associated with *me*, and may not be of interest to everyone.

Theory of mind is critical for having a successful conversation. While it may appear that conversations take place only to convey information, they are, in fact, a form of social engagement. When initiating a conversation with someone, we need to first convey to the other person that we are someone worth conversing with. Second, we need to convey how we feel about the other person with whom we are conversing. These are the implicit rules of conversation. Children with ASD do not understand the implicit rules behind having a conversation, and therefore this needs to be explained to them explicitly.

My goal when working with children with ASD is to help them understand that to be successful in a conversation, they need to show the other person "I like you" as well as convey information, and to ensure that the other person "likes me" so that she will listen. Thus, ToM is crucial for interactive conversation. For example:

I love Harry Potter. I love everything about Harry Potter. You come to me with your dinosaur collection. An honest, but inappropriate response would be, "I don't care about dinosaurs." For me, that statement is accurate and factual; it conveys what

I think about dinosaurs. But it also is conveying that I don't like you. A true conversation requires showing I like you even as you raise a topic that I am not interested in, and I raise a topic that you aren't interested in.

In the above situation, a more appropriate response would be:

> "Oh, that looks cool. I've never been into dinosaurs much, but I know a lot of people are really into dinosaurs."

This conveys that I am acknowledging your interest and not making a judgment about what you are interested in, and validates your perspective by acknowledging that, while I may not share your interest, I understand others do share your interest. This is showing the concept of "liking" as well as a need to be liked by the other person.

Once I've conveyed that I like you, then I can tell you what I like:

> "I love Harry Potter. Do you like Harry Potter?"

The initial statement tells you what I like, while the second question shows ToM: that my interest may or may not be the same as yours. By asking the question, I am engaging with you, not just talking at you. You may reply, "Yes," or you may reply, "No." The yes or no response is not important; what matters is that we are now mutually engaged in a conversation.

Another example of using ToM to engage in conversation:

> You just applied for a part in a play and didn't get it. You tell me, "I worked really hard to get that part, and didn't get it." It would be accurate, but inappropriate, if I responded, "I don't care about acting." An appropriate response would be, "You worked so hard; you should have gotten that part."

This is a very simple response. Essentially I just restated your statement back to you. But doing so conveys that I heard your feelings, as well as what you said, and that I care about you.

Children with ASD have decreased self-sight. Before we are able to have a true understanding about how others think and believe, we first have to have a deep understanding of ourselves. Children with ASD have difficulty separating themselves from others, and understanding that they have different strengths and weaknesses, beliefs and desires, and so on. Therefore, in therapy I try to stay away from the word "we" as this implies that we are one unit. Instead, I might say, "So you like dinosaurs and I like dinosaurs; we both like dinosaurs," in order to emphasize that the child and I are two separate persons who happen to share a common belief.

In a conversation I would say, "I like you and I know you like me, because you're a nice person and I'm a nice person." This conveys the same thought that we both like each other, but at the same time conveys that we are two separate people who happen to like each other.

This is crucial for those moments in our clinical sessions when I am causing the child stress during a challenging activity—she is able to think, "I like Miss Janice; she likes me. I'm a nice person; so is she. But right now Miss Janice is very annoying." This helps build the child's self-insight, her "other" perspectives, and her coping skills.

Teaching Theory of Mind

To teach ToM, start with a real-world example of how the child might feel in a situation.

> "How would you feel if you flunked a math test that you studied really hard for?"

A typical answer is, "I would feel really sad." As a clinician, I respond,

> "That's right! So how you would *feel* is how everyone else *feels*."

The "Sorry" Rule—Part of Theory of Mind

Responding to someone who says, "I'm sorry," is a variation of a conversation that also requires ToM. For example, when someone bumps into me when walking, that person typically will say, "I'm sorry." The appropriate response is a simple acknowledgement: "That's okay." A child with autism doesn't know that she needs to acknowledge the other person's apology. As a clinician, I need to explain explicitly that not responding communicates "I don't like you." When someone tells you, "I'm sorry," if you want to show the person that you like her, you need to say, "That's okay," or "No problem."

These seemingly simple situations all required advanced theory of mind development. These are all conversational rules we learned when we were very young by observing and practicing. Children with ASD need to be taught explicitly not just the rules, but the "why" behind the rules ("If I want people to know how fun, smart and wonderful I am, I have to... Otherwise people will think I don't like them").

CHAPTER 13

Teaching "Chit-Chat"

When we engage in "chit-chat," the back-and-forth questions and answers don't matter. Chit-chat is how we show others that we like them. Whether working with children or adults, I explicitly state this to the child or adult:

> "The only reason we have chit-chat is to show other people we like them. The answers don't matter."

I use chit-chat intentionally when I work with individuals with ASD. Whether children or adults, the word "conversation" has a very negative connotation for them—either they've been told numerous times that they are not good at conversations, or it's been part of a lesson (goal) in a therapy session. In many "conversation" lessons, the child is taught a script to say in response to a prompt: "Whenever someone says X, you respond Y."

Individuals on the spectrum do not have an understanding of either the purpose (function) or the structure of a social conversation. For example, verbal children on the spectrum will monologue to a person, without knowing that this is not a conversation. Neurotypical children have learned this implicitly; children on the spectrum need to be explicitly taught this.

When teaching chit-chat, I begin by explaining the chit-chat rule:

> "We're going to work on chit-chat. The first thing you need to know are the chit-chat rules. The first rule is that the only reason we do chit-chat is to show someone we like them; *in chit-chat the answers don't matter, we're just showing the other persons we like them.*"

I then go on to explain,

> "Before we are allowed to talk about what we want to talk about, *first* we have to show the other person we like them. The goal of chit-chat is to show the person we like them. Our face and our body have to show interest in the other person. That's how they know we like them.
>
> The second rule is the *pretend to care* rule. So no matter what the person says, you need to *pretend* to care. It's okay to pretend because the answers don't matter, the only thing that matters is showing the person you like them. So it's okay to pretend because that shows you like them."

Below is an example of how I introduce the chit-chat rules. The words in italics are my explanation to Billy about how the chit-chat works.

BILLY	JANICE
Hi Miss Janice.	Hi Billy.
How are you?	I'm fine. *Guess what: I'm not really fine, but I'm just pretending so that we can have chit-chat.*
How was your weekend?	I didn't do much; I just relaxed.
Oh, that's nice.	*Do you really care what I did on the weekend? [I shake my head to show "no."] No, you don't really care. But you pretended to care, by saying, "That's nice." Saying "That's nice" shows me you care, and that you like me.*

Here's another example.

BILLY	JANICE
Hi Miss Janice.	Hi Billy.
How are you?	I'm fine. *Guess what: I'm not really fine, but I'm just pretending so that we can have chit-chat.*
How was your weekend?	I went hiking!!
That sounds like fun!	*Maybe you don't really like to hike, but when you say, "That sounds like fun," you're showing the other person you like them and want to keep talking with them.* 　*Imagine you had said, "Yuck: I hate hiking!" Do you think the person would want to be your friend? Probably not—they don't know that you really like them because you didn't use the pretend to care rule.*

The above examples are not just to learn a "greeting" script, but to help the child understand that "greetings" are how we show others we like them.

Advanced "Chit-Chat": Asking and Answering Open-Ended Questions

Answering open-ended questions is critical to extending a conversation. For example, "How was school?" Many children with ASD struggle to answer this question. They may grow silent, or they might respond with something completely different from what the question asks. This is not because they won't answer it, but that they do not know how. Questions like "How was school?" can cause extreme dysregulation.

These children have no idea how to respond. They think there is a right answer, and they're afraid of giving a wrong answer.

I start with a casual question.

"How was school today?"

Then I patiently wait for *any* answer. I look for signs of dysregulation (stimming, fidgeting, etc.). Often, after a pause the child (let's call him Billy) might blurt out, "I had a math test," or "I had spaghetti for lunch." This answer tells me that Billy thinks there is a right answer— as if I am giving him a verbal test. Billy does not recognize that this question is really just part of chit-chat: how we have a conversation with others.

I then ask,

> "Am I going to call your principal? Do you think I care that you had a math test?"

As I ask these questions I shake my head, indicating "No." I want him to understand that asking a question is a sign that I like him. I don't care about the answer, and I need to make sure Billy understands this. What matters is not the answer, but rather that by asking the question, I am showing him that I care about the person I'm talking to.

To begin working on this, I start with a question that will cause the least amount of dysregulation, for example, about lunch or about recess. The first few times I do this typically require a lot of prompting on my part. I use a very friendly voice, not a question–answer voice; I want to convey that these interactions are about chit-chat and conversation, not about getting answers.

"Billy, what's one good thing that happened to you today?"

Then I wait for an answer... ["Lunch."]

> "Oh, that's good. I didn't have time to eat lunch today. When you had lunch today, what did you eat?"

Then I wait for an answer... ["Spaghetti."]

> "Do you like spaghetti? ['Yes.']
>
> I like spaghetti, too... [pause]
>
> So one good thing that happened to you today was...?"

Then I wait for a response, and if necessary, turn my ear to Billy to show that I am waiting for a response. If necessary I begin the sentence:

"One good thing that…"

I use prompting until Billy gives me a complete sentence ("One good thing that happened to me today was I had spaghetti for lunch.").

This single interaction can take a long time, especially at first. Depending on how Billy is responding, I may ask another question:

"What else happened to you today that was good?"

Then we repeat the process described above. If I see that this single interaction was stressful, I ask him if he needs a break.

"You look like you need a break. Do you need a break?"

The we start working on asking for a break. If he just nods, I prompt for a complete sentence, by turning my head. If he's still not answering I start prompting with the first few words of the sentence:

"Miss Janice, I…"

If he doesn't respond then I extend the prompt:

"Miss Janice, I need…"

We do this until he can tell me he needs a break in a full sentence, and then we stop so he can take a break. (While the child is taking a break—for example, playing with some toys in my office or playing on his computer tablet—I explain to the parent what just happened, and why I did what I did.)

I like to do chit-chat as naturalistically as possible. A natural time to do this is when the child first comes into the office; asking about your day is something that we say when we first see someone.

Over time, as the child becomes more able to tell me a good thing that happened without showing sign of dysregulation, thus demonstrating that this has become an emerging skill, I extend our chit-chat by asking about something that happened today that the child did *not* like. Again, with a friendly voice, I ask,

"Billy, tell me one thing that happened today that you *didn't* like?"

Remembering something that happened that he didn't like is likely to be stressful. The child is likely to be become silent, so I prompt.

"What about in school today? Was everything good at school today?"

I look for signs of dysregulation. As soon as I see signs of dysregulation I immediately ask, with a quizzical but friendly voice,

"Am I going to call your school? [Then I will prompt a 'no' response by shaking my head. ['No.'] Am I going to call your principal? ['No.']"

Then,

"Do I really *care* what happened at school?"

And I shake my head. Then,

"But I *do* like you. And I know you like me. This is how you show people how fun and smart you are. You ask them about their day. Do you care what they say? [I shake my head, no.] That's right. You don't care about the answer, but you do care about them. That's how you show them that you like them; you ask questions about their day."

Then I ask Billy to ask me how my day was, prompting as necessary:

Billy: "Miss Janice, how was your day?"

"Thank you for asking me. That's nice of you to ask me. Well, one good thing that happened to me today was…just before you and your mom came to see me, my husband sent me a text that he loved me.

One thing I didn't like was that our cat, Gingie, had a hairball and I had to clean it up before I came to work."

Depending on how I think Billy's feeling, I may then ask him a question:

"Do you have a pet at home?"

And we might do chit-chat about his pet.

In our back-and-forth chit-chat questions, I always refer to specific things that happened. For example, I may respond about something that happened at work, or at home. I want the child to understand that chit-chat conversations are about the person, not general good or bad things. Answers like "I liked today because it was warm" are not something that happened to him. If Billy gave me that answer, I would then say,

"Okay. but what happened at school today that you liked?"

Summary

We have these chit-chat conversations to start each session. The questions or topics will be different each time. Thus there is no one question–response script I want Billy to learn. Rather I am helping him develop a chit-chat protocol, or rules he can use with any questions or with any person. The rules are: (1) chit-chat is how we show someone we like them—the answers don't matter; and (2) we need to *pretend* we care, because that's how we show the other person we care about him and want to be friends.

The chit-chat interactions are also stimulating Billy's neural problem-solving activity:

- *Pause and reflect:* When I ask, "How was your day?" he needs to stop and think before answering.

- *Previously learned knowledge:* He has to think about what he likes and doesn't like.

- *Choice-making:* He has to choose what to talk about, and draw from his like/don't like mental categories.

- *In-depth vocabulary:* He has to put together full sentences that make sense.

- *Mental state/emotion vocabulary:* As we extend our chit-chat, I may ask him what annoyed him today, and he will need to give an answer that reflects annoyed, not irate or mad.

- *Asking for help:* This may happen when he's stuck, and I want him to remember to ask for help when he can't answer a question.

Part IV

LITERACY DEVELOPMENT

I cannot live without books.

Thomas Jefferson

CHAPTER 14

Developing Emerging Literacy Skills

The cognitive skill sets required for reading comprehension are the same as those required for higher-level thinking. Whether reading to understand fiction or nonfiction, readers rely on inner speech, comparing and contrasting what is read to what they must retrieve from prior knowledge, theory of mind, and so on. For this reason, I incorporate reading comprehension into my therapy sessions. Developing expressive or receptive language is required for reading comprehension, and vice versa.

Reading comprehension involves more than just being able to fluently read words on a page. There are different types of text for different genres, for example narrative text has a story structure—a beginning, a middle and an end—and there may or may not be illustrations. Narrative text includes literature or prose. Typically in fiction, the reader is generally required to understand the values, goals, motivation, emotions and reactions of the story's protagonist. In contrast, nonfiction (expository) reading is fact based. The expectations for the reader are different. With expository reading, the reader is expected to find or acquire information for future use. Expository reading includes textbooks in math, science, social studies, etc.

In this chapter we begin with basic decoding skills, and then move on to developing narrative (fiction) reading skills. In Chapter 15, we focus on expository (nonfiction) reading.

Teaching Children with ASD to "Decode" Words

When working on reading I separate decoding from comprehension. I emphasize that "'reading' is sounds, not 'letters.'" Often, educational curricula focus on letter names (e.g. the "ABC Song") and on spelling. Children with ASD are sometimes good spellers, but struggle with decoding.

Developing Decoding Skills: Helping Mary Become a Reader

When Mary was brought to me she was nine years old and a struggling reader; she needed help with decoding, and with reading comprehension. For example, she could not decode complex multi-syllabic words that did not have a 1:1 letter–sound correspondence.[1] Words like "traumatic" (trau-ma-tic) or "transportation" (trans-por-ta-shun) or even "enough" (e-nuff) are examples of complex, multi-syllabic words. Mary did not enjoy reading, in fact she "hated it."

The typical font size found in textbooks also adds to the complexity of decoding; the brain has to work harder to decipher the letters. This is why I always use a dry erase board when helping children with decoding. Making the letters larger makes them easier to process, and eases the cognitive load of decoding.

When working on decoding complex, multisyllabic words, I choose a book that is above the child's reading ability, so as to focus on decoding and not comprehension. I have found poetry books especially useful for this.

When Mary comes to a word she is having difficulty decoding (e.g. "negotiation"), we stop reading and I pull out the dry erase board and turn the book over to help her turn her attention to the dry erase board. I write on my dry erase board,

<u>ne</u>

1

and say,

"This is two letters; one sound. How do we read this?"

If Mary responds with an "n" and a short "e" ("neh"), or a long "e" ("nee"), I respond,

---

1   "Bat" is an example of a word with a 1:1 letter–sound correspondence.

"That was a great guess, Mary. You're right; it should be a 'neh' [or 'nee']. The sound does not match the letter. And that makes it tricky. It's not fair that it's not a 'neh,' but English is hard. That's why it feels hard, because it is.

It's actually read, 'nuh.' So how do we read this?"

And then I wait for Mary to respond.
Then I write,

$$\underset{2}{\underline{go}}$$

And then ask,

"How do we read this?"

And when Mary reads "go," I praise her for reading "go."
Then I write,

$$\underset{3}{\underline{ti}}$$

And say,

"For this one, I'm going to help you because the sound doesn't match the letters; you just have to memorize it. So I will read it first."

And point to it, and read,

"'she'… So Mary, how do we read this?"

I have Mary read "she" when looking at "ti" several times.
Then I write,

$$\underset{4}{\underline{a}}$$

Then I point to the "a" and ask her how we read this.

If she responds with the short sound, I say, "We need the long sound." If she is not able to retrieve the long sound, I prompt by asking, "What is the name of this letter?" This is the *only* time I will refer to the word "letter" versus "sound." Once she says the letter name, I state, "Yes, that's how we read this. So how do we read this?" and wait for her to respond accordingly.

tion
ɔ

The suffix "tion" occurs frequently in the English language, particularly in academic settings. For this reason, I spend extra time helping the child learn this. I being with:

> "This is one sound, four letters; we read this as 'shun.' That's not fair is it? I want to know who made this rule."

The child always agrees with me, because if one thinks about it, it's *not* fair.

> "So I'm going to help you. We read this as 'shun.' Now we are going to say this back and forth five times, because that's the only way our brain learns. I wish learning was fun, but it's not. We call everything we do the first time 'hard.' The only way we can call this 'easy' is to practice. I will go first."

I then say slowly,

> "'t-i-o-n' is 'shun.'"

Then Mary repeats, "'t-i-o-n' is 'shun.'" We repeat this five or six times in order for her to process this into long-term memory. Then I turn the book over and state,

> "Find the word in the book; then read it."

Once she finds it and reads it without difficulty—"negotiation"—we continue reading until the next word she has trouble decoding. The process is repeated using the dry erase board with the new word.

It is important to note that when working on decoding, I do *not* also work on comprehension. I treat decoding and reading comprehension as separate and distinct goals. Typically, when teaching decoding, I will use a book of poetry rather than a book of prose. Poetry contains infrequently used words, or unusual words, and often requires more complex decoding. This helps both the child and me stay focused on decoding and pronunciation, rather than on comprehension.

Teaching Reading Comprehension to Children with ASD

Reading comprehension requires active and ultimately very complex problem-solving. Reading comprehension at the most basic level is understanding vocabulary. Proficient readers are actively making sense of what they read. They retrieve their in-depth vocabulary knowledge, grammar, sentence structure and world knowledge. Readers compare and contrast the text in front of them with their world knowledge and are then able to comprehend what they are reading. For proficient readers, this happens almost instantaneously.

Because reading comprehension involves complex problem-solving, it is no wonder that children with ASD struggle with reading comprehension. Below are the different components that I work on to facilitate reading comprehension.

Using a "Reading Finger"

When Yvonne came to me she had basic decoding ability but only minimal reading comprehension skills. I started with very early reading books that have only one sentence per page, such as picture books. I teach children to use their "reading finger" (using the index finger to point to each word). This will require Yvonne to slow down, and look at each word as we read them.

Immediate visual recall is usually a strength for children on the spectrum. They often memorize the first sentence, and recite it back without looking at the book. When I recognize this, I tell them, "That's not reading; that's talking." And while tapping words, I say, "Reading is words. If you're not looking at the words, you're not reading. Let me know when you're ready; I need your reading finger."

I place the picture book in front of Yvonne, and explain that we are going to read the book together; I will read and she will follow along with her reading finger. My goal is to help Yvonne *think* about the words we are reading. Therefore I read slowly and deliberately, and as

I read, Yvonne has to use her reading finger to point to each word as I read it. I do not allow her to move her finger until I am completely done reading each word. If I see that she is not pointing to each word as I am reading it, I immediately stop and say,

"Wait, I haven't finished reading the word yet."

Then we continue, while making sure Yvonne follows each word with her reading finger as I read each word. This process helps her slow down so she can keep her focus on each word.

Finding the Important Words in a Sentence

Children with ASD often need help making sense of the words they are reading. My goal is to help them actively think about each word they read. Proficient readers are always comparing and contrasting their world knowledge with what they are reading.

I begin by reading the first sentence in the book, for example:

"The boy went to the store."
After reading it, I turn to Yvonne and say,

"Now we need to know what the important words are. These tell us what the story is about. I'm going to be your secretary. I'm going to write down everything you say because we need to make a list of all the important words. That will tell us what the story is about."

If Yvonne merely reads back the entire sentence, I then prompt with,

"That was great reading, but it doesn't tell me what the important words are. What do you think the first important word is?"

If Yvonne points to a word in the middle of the sentence (*went*) or at the end of the sentence (*store*), I prompt:

"No, you missed some words. You need to go all the way back to the beginning of the sentence. Where's the beginning of the sentence?"

I help her by putting her finger on "The" and say,

"Is 'the' important?"

If she says, "Yes" (which at first often happens), I say,

"Can we see 'the'? Can we hold 'the'?"

And I might shake my head to help her answer, "No." Then I say,

"That's right; 'the' is *not* an important word."

Then I say,

"Is 'boy' important?"

When Yvonne says, "Yes," I say,

"Yes, that's right. 'Boy' is important."

Using my dry erase board, I write the word "boy" and place a tally mark next to it:

boy |

We then do this for each important word in the sentence.

went |

store |

Then we continue to read the story, with her using her reading finger as I read the sentence in the book. Each time we get to a different important word in a sentence, I write it down and place a tally mark next to it. But each time one of the important words is repeated, we add another tally mark to the word. Over the course of the story, "boy" keeps appearing, so "boy" will have multiple tally marks.

boy ||||

When we come across a pronoun for the boy ("he"), I ask Yvonne,

"Who is 'he'?"

and wait for her to say, "The boy." Then I say,

"That's right, 'he' is 'the boy.' So I'm going to put another tally mark next to 'boy.'"

This helps Yvonne learn to use pronouns (e.g. "he") to refer back to the subject of the story, in this case "the boy," when reading.

When we finish reading the story, I show her the dry erase board and say,

"Okay, I'm your secretary. Tell me which words have the most tallies and I'll write them down."

For this example, I might write,

boy

store

milk

and then say,

"Now, tell me what the story is about."

I help Yvonne construct a sentence using the words with the most tally marks, such as "The story is about a boy going to the store to get some milk," and then say to her,

"Yes, that's right. Great reading. The story is about a boy going to the store to get some milk."

Yvonne and I did this over many months. Gradually we moved on to more complex books.

Complex Reading Comprehension

Understanding Characters' Intent, Motivation and Emotions

From simple stories, we progress to more complex stories. When reading literature, the reader has to understand the intentions and motivations of the characters. This requires the reader to retrieve her world knowledge of any situation that seems remotely similar to the situation in the book, and then project this intention on to the character in the book. That is, the reader actively pulls up her world knowledge, and compares and contrasts her experiences with that of the character in the story, and conclude that the character would do what she, the reader, would do.

The same process is used for emotion questions. For example, in a story about a girl who was hoping to get a puppy for her birthday and didn't, when asked, "Why do you think Sally was so sad?" readers pull up their world knowledge about how they felt when they ended up not getting what they wanted on their birthday. That is, readers actively pull up their world knowledge, and compare and contrast their feelings in a similar situation to that of the character, Sally, and conclude that the character would feel as they would.

Projecting emotion or intent requires theory of mind, which is a hallmark deficit of children on the spectrum.[2] As a result, they need explicit instruction to help them learn how to answer a question about how a character in a story feels, which requires projecting a feeling from their own experience on to that of the character. Children with autism typically assume that they have to know the character in the book to know how the character would feel. They literally have no idea how to answer the question.

When working with Yvonne, I begin with our joint reading experience, with me reading and Yvonne following along with her finger. Using the example about the girl who didn't get a puppy for her birthday, I ask Yvonne,

"Why do you think Sally is so sad?"

When I see she's not going to be able to answer the question, I prompt Yvonne with exaggerated facial and verbal expressions:

"How would you feel if you wanted a puppy and didn't get one? How would you feel?" [looking sad]

Picking up the cue, Yvonne answers, "Sad."
Then I quickly respond in an animated and exaggerated voice,

---

2 As described previously, ToM first requires self-sight about one's own emotions and intentions in different situations. With self-insight about my own feelings, I can then compare and contrast the character's situation with similar experiences I had, recognize that I felt sad, and then project this emotion on to the character in the story. This is both an analytic compare and contrast process and an emotional one.

"Yes! That's right! The answer for you is the right answer for how Sally feels, too! That's how we answer book questions! You know all the right answers!"

Knowing that this kind of question about emotion is likely to cause dysregulation, my vocal and expressive prompting is important for reassurance, as well as providing explicit praise for what the child did. Explicit instruction teaches the child:

- she does not have to know the character to answer the question

- how she feels in any given situation is the answer for how the character would feel in the same situation, and therefore

- the child already has the answer: she needs to think about how she would feel, and use that knowledge to answer the question about the character in the story.

Using Reading Literature to Develop Theory of Mind

When Yvonne turned 11 years old, her parents wanted me to help her with a biography book they were reading at school about the life of Helen Keller. Helen Keller was born in 1880. She became blind and deaf at 19 months after contracting an illness. In 1887 Helen's mother hired Anne Sullivan, a student of Alexander Graham Bell, who was herself visually impaired, to be her teacher. The book describes the relationship between Helen and Anne Sullivan, and how Anne Sullivan helped Helen to learn to communicate and to read.

I used this story to focus on understanding perspectives of more than one protagonist, in this case Anne Sullivan and Helen Keller. Reading literature is an opportunity to help children with ASD develop their theory of mind (ToM). Theory of mind requires that the child learn that what someone else knows may be different from what the child knows.

ToM also requires the child to see the world from the perspective of someone else. To do this, one must first have self-insight, including understanding one's own emotions and what causes them. Then, one's self-insight is compared and contrasted with that of another person. Self-insight, understanding one's own emotions, understanding the emotions of someone else, comparing and contrasting one's own emotions with someone else's emotions, and understanding *why* one's own emotions are different than someone else's requires a great deal of cognitive effort. This is a complex problem-solving task for children with ASD. It involves both an analytic compare-and-contrast process (what I know versus what another person knows), and an emotional compare-and-contrast process (what I feel versus what another person feels).

However, this cognitive task becomes appreciably more complex when it involves more than one character, neither of whom are one's self. Take, for, example two very basic question to ask from this book:

> "When Annie first came to the house, how do you think Helen felt?"

and

> "How do you think Annie felt?"

Understanding feelings requires having well-developed emotional state vocabulary: the ability to assign different labels to different feelings, and different labels for differing *levels* of intensity for the same general category of feelings, first for one's self and then for the other person, or persons.

In the case of, "How do you think Helen felt?" Yvonne is required to:

- find or remember that portion of the book

- infer a feeling that Helen might have based on the situation described in the book

- infer a feeling, presumably different, that Annie might have had based on the same situation in the book.

Inferring Helen's feeling requires Yvonne to put herself in the situation of Helen, and realize that how she would feel is how Helen probably feels.

CHAPTER 15

Understanding and Reading Textbooks

Regardless of the topic, all textbooks share common components and organization. Before we even open a textbook, we have retrieved from our world knowledge information that alerts us that this is a textbook. We know that it will have a table of contents, a title page that includes both the topic of information and the author, and a front and back cover that may give additional clues to the content. We prepare ourselves to read to learn facts, information, and so on. We know this from our years of experience in classes that used textbooks.

Children with ASD have limited ability to store and retrieve their world knowledge and use it to make assumptions: that is, to use world knowledge to infer more about the information or resource in front of them. Unless they are explicitly taught, in general they neither learn by observing nor make inferences beyond what they just learned. Thus, children with ASD will learn that the book they are currently looking at has a table of contents, but they are not likely to generalize this to every textbook they will encounter in the future. Thus, children with ASD will learn that the book they are currently looking at has a table of contents, but they are not likely to generalize this to every textbook they will encounter in the future. They need to be taught the structure of a textbook first, and understand that this structure will be the same for every textbook, not just the textbook in front of them. Understanding the structure and components of a textbook needs to become embedded in their world knowledge. Too often, I have found that even children with Asperger's syndrome who have been mainstreamed are very inefficient at understanding how to use a textbook.

Intervention

I start by asking what classes they are taking at school. Typical answers are social studies, reading (or language arts), science, and math (or arithmetic). We then talk about the difference between their language arts books and the books in their other classes. My goal is to have the children think about the subject matter in their classes, including thinking about the differences: that is, comparing and contrasting between their fact-based classes (science, math and social studies) and their language arts class.

To introduce nonfiction reading, I begin by asking questions (often receiving incorrect responses).

"In your reading class, what are your stories about?

Do they have maps? ['No.']

Do they have diagrams or charts? ['No.']

Do they have a lot of numbers? ['No.']

That's right!

What about places, or vegetables, or trees? ['No.']"

Then I ask,

"*Who* are they about? Are they about people?"

I will nod up and down, to prompt them to say "People."

"That's right; they are about people."

Then I ask,

"Are they ever about animals?"

Some children might respond, "Yes. [book] is a story about a fox that is looking for a buried treasure…"

"That's right, sometimes stories are about animals. What about in your science class; are there animals in your textbook?" ["Yes."]

Then I ask,

"So, in your science textbook, do the animals act like people, like trying to find buried treasure? ['No.']

You're right. They describe where they live, or what they eat, or show a picture of the parts of the animal."

Then we discuss what they have learned in one of their textbooks, and I write down what they say on my dry erase board. For example, if it's about an animal, I write down where they live, what they eat, and so on. This gives me a starting point to talk about their fact-based classes.

Whatever topic they've talked about, I transition to one of my books that's from the same general area. For example, if it's a topic from a science class, I take a book with science information, open it in the middle and we go through as I point out different parts of the book.

"Look, there's a diagram showing different parts of a dog."

On my dry erase board, I write down, "diagram."

"Look at the diagram. It has labels pointing to different parts of the dog. That's how we know it's a diagram, it has labels on the picture."

I am helping the child have a visual picture of what a diagram is. Then we turn through some more pages until I see something else: "There's a chart"; "There's a graph"; "There's a diagram of a different animal." And for each different figure (graph, chart, diagram, etc.), I write the name of that figure on my dry erase board, and explain what it is. Then, pointing to the words on the dry erase board, I say,

"So how do we know it's a science book? Because it has diagrams, and charts, and graphs."

Then I take out a different kind of textbook, and go through the same process. For example, in an arithmetic book, we'll go through and find graphs and tables, maybe formulas, and, of course, lots and lots of numbers. Again, I use my dry erase board and list what we find— numbers, tables, graphs, and so on—explaining what makes it a table or a graph or a chart. ("A graph or table or chart tells you how many things there are.") Then, pointing to the words on the dry erase board:

"So, how do we know it's a math book? Because it has lots of numbers, and tables of numbers, and graphs."

Then I turn to the last subject, social studies, and do the same thing, pointing out maps and pictures of people, and so on, and explaining what they are and why they're there. ("A map tells you *where* things happen. Social studies is the only class where you learn *where* something happens.") As before, I point to the labels that I've written on my dry erase board, and say,

> "That's how we know it's a social studies textbook. It has maps, and pictures of people."

This is how I introduce the concept of "textbooks." My goal is to help them process into their rote memory not just the labels (map, chart, diagram, etc.) but also what they mean in their own words. For example, I might make a game of it:

"What's a…map?"

"What's a…diagram?"

Additionally, I might show them a picture of a map or a chart and ask them, "What's that?" (child answers, "A map"), then I ask, "How do you know?" Then, I wait for the child to answer, helping him if needed.

My goal is to help children use their own words to process in explicit language (their own) what these different things in textbooks are. This depends on them understanding that they are able to actively think about what they're reading. My goal is not for them to learn the textbook definition; I want them to process these concepts in their own words. This creates active thinking on their part when utilizing textbooks.

I start with any nonfiction or textbook in my office that is age appropriate. Examples of books I have used are *Health and Growth* or *American Presidents*. It doesn't matter if it is an actual textbook or not, as long as it has the basic features of a textbook. However, I do not use a textbook from the child's school, as I want to start with a book the child is not familiar with.

I put the book in front of the child, and ask,

> "I wonder what class you would read this in?
>
> I wonder how many pages it has?
>
> I wonder if it has an index?"

I start with "I wonder" because I do *not* want this to sound like a quiz. Instead I want this to feel like a conversation. However, for me this is an informal assessment to learn what the child knows about using a textbook. When he tells me the class he would read it in (science, history, etc.), I might probe and ask why he said what he did. When I ask about the number of pages, I watch to see if the child turns to the back (many don't) or starts turning the pages one by one. I also want to see if he knows where to find a page number on the page. When I ask about the index, I want to see if he knows what it is, or how to find it. I use these questions to understand what the child already knows; I do not want to spend time on what he knows, only what he doesn't.

Teaching "How to Use a Textbook": Billy

Billy is a middle-school student who has never been explicitly taught how to use a textbook. I begin by talking with him about the structure of the book. We start with the front and back covers, and talk about any pictures or written descriptions that appear. I use these pictures or descriptions to begin talking about the topic of the book, noting that they cue us that this a science book, or a math book, or a social studies book.

Below is the list of the parts of the textbook that I will explicitly go over with the child. This is not an all-inclusive list, but are the main sections I will discuss:

- table of contents
- heading
- chapter
- subheading
- introduction
- bold print and italicized print
- index
- glossary (if appropriate).

Defining each of these terms is a separate activity that Billy and I do together. The definitions I use may not be precisely accurate; my goal is to make the meanings as concrete as possible. I therefore use descriptors and phrases that help him visualize what these terms mean, and to retain verbal descriptions he can think about when needing to read and understand a textbook.

Table of Contents

I begin with the table of contents. I write it on my dry erase board and explain what the table of contents is, and end with a question:

> "The table of contents tells me where things are in the book so that I don't have to look through the entire book for something. Where in this textbook could I find the table of contents?"

Some children will know: "At the beginning." Others need help coming up with the right answer. I then go page by page through the beginning of the book, explaining the title page, pointing out the author, the date it was published, and so on, until I get to the table of contents.

Often in textbooks, there is no page labeled "Table of Contents"; instead it will read "Contents." When the child reads, "Contents," I respond,

> "That's right. This is the table of contents. The table of contents tells us where the chapters are."

Then I close the book and ask him,

> "How many chapters are in this book?"

Often children like Billy will proceed to go through the book looking for chapters. That's my cue that they do not understand how to use the table of contents. I have him find the table of contents, remind him what the table of contents is and ask him again, "How many chapters are in this book?" Even with the book open at the table of contents (or "Contents") I can get different answers. Some children pick up on the "how many" and look for a *number* (a typical answer for a "how many" question), and will read a page number out loud instead of counting the number of chapters. In this case, I have to explain that the page number is where the chapter starts, but it is not the total number of chapters. Others will count everything, including sections that are not chapters, such as the introduction in the beginning and the index at the end. In these cases, I need to explain the difference between a chapter and the introduction and the index, explain what each of these is, and then ask again how many *chapters* there are. I may need to repeat this and provide descriptions and explanations about the difference until they give me the right number of chapters. I also explain what the numbers are—that is, the first page of each chapter.

Then I again close the book, and ask Billy to tell me what page Chapter 5 begins on. Billy may start going through the book page by page to find Chapter 5. If so, I redirect him to the table of contents, restate what the table of contents is ("The table of contents tells us where the chapters are"), show him where the page number next to the chapter title is, and explain what it is and why it is there. With the table of contents open, I ask him at what page Chapter 5 begins.

Then I ask him to find Chapter 5 in the book. I watch to see how Billy searches for Chapter 5. For example, does he again go page by page, or does he "scan" page numbers? In some cases, I have to show a child how to find a chapter in the middle of the book, for example:

"Take a bunch of pages like this, and what page are you on now?"

The child might only take a few pages; that's fine. I tell him, "Keep going."

Sometimes in taking a bunch of pages, the child will pass by the first page of the chapter, and when the child realizes this he starts to dysregulate: "I missed it!" ("end of the world" reaction). When that happens I calmly respond,

"That's okay. We just go back."

Often children's initial reaction is to close the book and start over; they repeat the process from the beginning because they think, "I got it wrong; I have to start all over again." They are not yet able to recognize that this is all part of the problem-solving search process, in which the next step is merely to count pages backwards; they have not internalized that this is a process: "I just need to count the pages backwards until I reach the beginning of the chapter"). Instead they are doing what they're used to doing, treating it as an activity which they got wrong (and thus must start over again).

When this happens, I help them by prompting them to just take a bunch of pages to go backwards. This may take some time because they may only want to take one or two pages at a time for fear that they might "miss it" again. If so, that's fine. I do not want to discourage them. My goal throughout this activity is teach them how to use a textbook: that is, find things. We are not actually reading the book, only learning how to search through a textbook.

After explaining the table of contents, I then move on to understanding how a textbook is structured, so they can find information in the book.

Heading

I typically start with headings. Using another dry erase board, I write down "Heading," and ask,

"What word in here do you see?"

When Billy answers, "Head," I underline it, and respond,

"Right. Where on the body is a head?"

$$\underline{\text{Hea}}\text{ding}$$

If I see that Billy isn't sure what to answer, I might prompt,

"Is the head at the top of the body?"

When Billy says, "Yes," I respond,

"That's right. The head is on the top the body. So let's find a *heading* in the book. Where do you think you'd find a *heading* in the book?"

I then open the book anywhere and we go through page by page until we find a heading. For instructional purposes I initially verbally label chapter titles as "headings." When I come to one, I say,

"Look, it's on the top of the page, just like a head is on the top of the body. A heading is the title of the chapter. A heading is how you know what the chapter is about."

Then I close the book, open it anywhere, and help Billy find another heading. We do this several times, until I see he's able to do it on his own. As we do this, I describe what makes the heading different than the rest of the text: its size (larger font), and whatever else makes it stand out: for example some are bold, some are italics, and some are in a different font style.

Chapter

To explain what a chapter is, I write "Chapter" on the dry erase board and say,

> "Books are broken down into sections called 'chapters.' Each chapter is about a 'topic.' A 'topic' is what the chapter is about."

Then I show Billy several chapters, including holding the several pages that make up each chapter.

Subheading

I then turn to the next word on our list, and we talk about "subheading." Using the other dry erase board, I write down "Sub-heading," and ask,

> "What words do you see?"

Subheading contains two words, *sub* and *head*. I start with whichever one Billy says first, underline it and then ask what other word he sees, and underline it. On the dry erase board, I'll have written,

$$\underline{Sub} \ \underline{heading}$$

Then I ask,

> "What do you think 'sub' means?"

I pause, and if he doesn't say anything I state,

> "Like a *sub*marine; a *sub*marine goes *under* the water."

I move one of my hands under the other arm to show "under," and say,

> "Yeah, 'sub' means *under*. I wonder where on the page, a *sub*heading
> would be. Do you think it will be *over* the heading or *under* the
> heading?" ["Under."]

Then I add the words "under" and "top" to the dry erase board.

> "Okay, so let's look for a subheading. A *sub*heading is about a
> smaller part of a chapter. It is *under* a heading."

At this point, I also explain bold and italics. I explain that:

> "Headings and subheading are usually *bold* or *italics*. That's how
> you know they are headings or subheadings. 'Bold' means the
> print is darker, 'italics' means the writing is slanted."

I draw on a dry erase board a slanted line and a straight line, so that
Billy can see what I mean by "slanted."

/ |

Then I open up the book to any page, and starting at the top of the
page, use his reading finger to scan the page looking for a subheading.
If we get to the bottom of the page, and there is no subheading, I
ask Billy,

> "Are there any subheadings on the page?"

I prompt by shaking my head, until he says, "No." Starting at the top
of the next page we continue scanning with his finger. When we get
to a subheading (italics or bold), I wait for Billy to stop and tell me
he's found a subheading, or I point to it, and ask,

> "Is this a subheading?"

while nodding to prompt him to say, "A subheading." If he only nods or says, "Yes," I ask him what it's called. I want him to verbalize "subheading" to facilitate long-term retention. We will do this until he says "subheading" consistently.

While we're scanning, if we come to a heading, I ask,

"Is this a 'subheading'?"

I am hoping he'll say, "No," and I'll then ask him what it is ["A heading."]; I may need to shake my head as a prompt, until he says, "No," and then ask him what it is. Either on his own or with a prompt, Billy will state, "Heading," and I respond,

"Right! It's a heading. Let's keep going until we find a subheading."

Introduction

I write "Introduction" on the dry erase board, along with "Intro":

Then I ask,

"When do we introduce ourselves to someone? Do we introduce ourselves at the end of our conversation?"

When Billy answers, "No, at the beginning," I then ask,

"So…where do think you'll find the introduction? ['At the beginning.'] So let's see if it's at the beginning of the book."

I open the book towards the beginning, and when we see the introduction, I respond,

"Yes, here it is; it's at the beginning of the book. Just like when we introduce ourselves to someone new."

We finish with the index and the glossary.

Index

"An index tells you where important words are."

Then I show Billy the index, and show him how to use the index to find an important word in the textbook.

Glossary

"A glossary is like a dictionary; it tells you what a word means."

Scanning for Information

Unlike when we read fiction, when we read nonfiction we are reading for information. Finding answers in a nonfiction book requires visual scanning; we scan text to find the answers to questions. Research shows that children with ASD are not good at visual scanning. Even children with ADHD scan more efficiently than children with autism. Therefore, before they are able to scan text for finding information, children with autism need to be taught *how* to scan.

I am no longer surprised at the number of children with autism who have no idea how to scan. To get a sense of whether a child knows how to scan, I will open a book and ask a question from the page, and tell the child to use the reading finger to scan the page to find the answer. Some children will put their finger in the middle of page, some will put it at the end of the page, and some will appropriately start at the beginning—the upper left-hand corner of the page. I have worked with children ranging from mainstream to self-contained classes who have never explicitly been taught how to scan. What I see is a random process. Even very verbal children with autism may not know how to scan proficiently, by starting at the upper left-hand side of the page. The only way I know how proficient a scanner they are is to specifically observe what they do.

The Case of Charles—An Inefficient Scanner

A quick, informal way to assess a child's ability to scan is to have him read a paragraph of text silently at whatever reading level is appropriate for the child, and see how long it takes for him to look up.

For example, if I think it would take about 15 seconds to read for understanding, and Charles looks up after five seconds, it suggests that Charles is an inefficient scanner. He is an *inefficient* scanner because he is done too quickly to have gleaned any useful information from the passage.

When this happens, I turn to the child and say,

> "That should have taken you about 15 seconds; you took only 5 seconds. Your brain is going too fast. So I'm going to teach you how to slow your brain down."

When I work on scanning, I am only working on the psychomotor processes required for visually attending to the passage in front of the child. I do not simultaneously work on either decoding or comprehension. To show Charles how to scan, I put my finger on the first word of the paragraph on a page, slowly move from the beginning of the first sentence to the end, then do the same for the second sentence, and continue for the entire paragraph. I then have Charles do the same thing. If he is not sure what to do, I may take his finger, and have him do the same thing I did: slowly move his finger from the beginning of the first sentence to the end, then do the same for the second sentence, and continue for the entire paragraph. I work on this until Charles can move his finger without my assistance. Then I praise Charles:

> "Charles, that was great scanning! What a great scanner you are! You are scanning all by yourself. You don't need anybody's help. You can scan all by yourself!"

I am not expecting Charles to read. My focus is only on the physical movement; I want him to understand the motion of scanning. Just this psychomotor activity of moving one's finger across a page requires cognitive resources to keep one's eyes on each word, moving from word to word, sentence to sentence, until the end of the paragraph.

In the beginning, his scanning is too fast. To help him slow down, I say,

> "Oh, you're going too fast; let me help you."

I then hold his finger and guide it from left to right.

To further refine his scanning ability, I take a book that I know he can decode, and we take turns reading (decoding) and scanning.

I place the book in front of Charles, and explain that we are going to read the book together; I will read and he will follow along with his reading finger. My goal is to help Charles begin to *think* about the words we are reading. I read slowly and deliberately, and as I read, Charles has to use his reading finger to point to each word as I read it. I do not allow him to move his finger until I am completely done reading each word. If I see that he is not pointing to each word as I read it, I immediately stop and say,

"Wait, I haven't finished reading the word yet."

The process is slow; regardless of who is reading and who is using his reading finger to follow along, I am structuring this activity so that we go word by word. I am also peripherally checking to see if Charles's eyes are on the words I am reading or are drifting away; I want to make sure that Charles follows each word with his reading finger as I read each word. This process helps Charles slow down so he can keep his focus on each word. Scanning is an essential first step in being able to find an answer in a text.

CHAPTER 16

Note Taking, Teaching Time and Assisting with Arithmetic

Note Taking

In addition to neurocognitive deficits, children with ASD often have motor deficits which make handwriting effortful and very tiring. In early grades where children learn to write, and good penmanship is emphasized, they may either avoid writing or need to spend additional time (because of the additional effort) making sure their handwriting is legible. One "rule" they may take from these early years of handwriting instruction is that handwriting needs to be legible. Handwriting for these children becomes a slow and calligraphy-like activity. These "rules" about handwriting become barriers to good note taking.

In the classroom students need to take notes when listening to teachers, and when learning material in textbooks. But note taking is not just an academic skill, it is also a life skill. We write notes to ourselves in everyday life, for example grocery lists and to-do lists. Note taking is very different from academic writing. But rarely does anyone explicitly teach us the difference.

Note taking involves cryptic writing:

- leaving out articles and prepositions
- using abbreviations
- using symbols
- writing sloppily
- not worrying about spelling.

Teaching Note Taking

As has been described, much of my intervention is note taking. Sometimes it involves using the dry erase board to write down words, symbols, and so on; other times I take out an actual to-do pad, and use it to write the list of things we will work on. Thus the children I work with already have a foundation for understanding note taking, even though I have not explicitly explained what it is. As the child gets older, and especially by second or third grade when students begin to use "reading to learn" as opposed to learning to read, I begin explicit instruction on note taking.

I take out a to-do note pad and my pencil cup, and say,

"Okay, I'm going to take a pencil and I want you to take a pencil."

The reason I have the child take a pencil from the cup is because I want her to be actively engaged. Even if she ends up not actually writing, taking out a pencil and holding it during the note-taking process is activating the brain for "note taking."

TO-DO note-pad
♡ Chit-chat
🦉 Reading
♡ Q and A
🦉
♡
🦉
♡
🦉
♡

By third grade, I want the children to do what I do, so we both have a note pad and we both have a pencil. Then I list what we will be doing that day, and have them do the same thing on their note pad. For example, I might write "Chit-chat." I intentionally write it fast and sloppily. I watch what they do and as I see them begin to write carefully, I remind them that this is just for them so they can write the words "Chit-chat" sloppily, and I explicitly explain why when note taking it is okay to be a sloppy writer:

> "This is note taking, not school writing, so you want to do it fast and it's okay to be sloppy.
>
> Is this going to be graded? [I wait for the child to respond, 'No.']
>
> Is this going to be turned in to the teacher? [I wait for the child to respond, 'No.']"

The child writes down all the activities we will do that session. Where appropriate I encourage using just single words in place of a phrase or sentence, or abbreviations; these are what we use when taking notes. In the example provided, after chit-chat, we work on reading from a book; I write just "Reading." Likewise, I don't write "Questions and Answers," instead I write (and so do they) "Q and A."

We then start on the first activity of the list, chit-chat. When we're done I say,

> "That's all the chit-chat I have."

Then I wait for the child to say, "That's all the chit-chat I have." I want to hear a verbal response, because I want the child to actively engage her brain in verbalization.

At first, the child may not say it, so I nonverbally encourage her. I look at her and wait; I might raise my eyebrows to signal that it's the child's turn to talk. Then I might start the response I'm looking for by my saying as I look at her,

> "Miss Janice, that's...
>
> Miss Janice, that's all...
>
> Miss Janice, that's all the chit-chat...
>
> Miss Janice, that's all the chit-chat I have..."

I do this until she expresses that she is done, too. Not only is this activating her verbal pathways, it is also engaging in a dialogic interaction.

After she gives me a response, I say,

"Okay, we're all done with chit-chat; go check it off."

It's her job to check it off the list, and I wait for her to do it. Often children ask me,

"What should I do?"

or

"How do I do that?"

They say this because they don't want to be wrong; they don't want to make a mistake. If the child asks this, I respond,

"That's up to you. Do you want to use a check mark, or do you want to check it off? Whatever you want to do—it's up to you."

This serves two purposes. Subtly, I am forcing her to make a choice, one of the problem-solving processes. But my more overt goal is to have her *own* the activity as her own: it is her list, not mine; she can do what she wants because it is her note-taking list.

I wait for her to do whatever she chooses; then I ask,

"What's next on the list?"

We move to the next item on the list. The child looks at the list and responds, "Reading."

Then I say,

"Okay, now we're ready to read a book."

Then we start the next activity on the list.

When we're done, I throw the paper away, so she can see that no one else will see this; it is just for her. I'll wait for the child to do the same thing.

Teaching *"Using"* Time (Not "Telling" Time)

In today's world of digital clocks, telling time is rarely a problem for children on the autism spectrum. However, telling time, and understanding how to use time to answer a question are very different things. Examples of questions that require *using* time are:

"How much time is left before we stop?"

"How long do we have to do this?"

These questions require the child to manipulate the concept of time. Time is a difficult concept. We don't *see* time; it has no physical attributes. Yet time is very real, and everything in our lives seems to revolve around it.

Teaching Time

I always use a clock with manipulable hands to teach children to use time. I also have a large clock with hands on the wall in my office. Reading time on a clock with hands requires ignoring the numbers on the clock to read the minutes, while attending to the numbers to read the hour. On the clock face below, even though the minute hand is pointing at about '6,' it is referring to about 30 minutes. In contrast, the hour hand that is pointing to '8' is referring to '8.' For me to teach a child to answer time questions—to use time—the child needs to be able to count in fives; typically this is around ages seven or eight.

Teaching the Vocabulary of Time: "After" and "Till"

I take out a picture a clock and explain:

"From here to here (the 12 to the 6), we use the word 'after,' for example, 10 minutes after five."  "From here to here (the 12 to the 6), we use the word 'till,' for example, 15 minutes till four."

If they ask "why," I respond, "I don't know why we say this, it just is." Explaining how we use "till" and "after" when talking about time is a simple rule that these children can remember; "till" and "after" provide the child with explicit labels and descriptions for understanding how to use time, that is, to have language to begin figuring out "How many more minutes do I have before I get to go home?"

The use of time typically comes up during an activity, when the child starts to get tired or antsy. The child will often look up at the clock, or she might say (often in a whining voice), "How much longer is this?"

When this happens, I stop, and then say,

> "I'm going to help you figure it out. "Do you know how to count by fives?"

First, we practice counting by fives together. Then I take out my manipulable clock, put her finger on the '1' and say "Five," then move her finger to the '2' and say "Ten"; we continue this until we get to the '12' and I say "Sixty." Then I ask,

> "So, how many minutes are there in an hour? There are 60 minutes in an hour."

Typically, we do this a few times to make sure I know the child understands that when counting on the clock we are not referring to the number, but to increments of five minutes, and can correctly respond "60" when I ask how many minutes are in an hour.

Then I move the hands of my clock to match the time on my wall clock. Then I explain how to count the time on the clock. Using the picture of the clock on the previous page, if my session started at eight o'clock and went on to nine o'clock, I explain,

"We start with the number after the big hand, and count by fives. So how much time is left?"

And putting her finger on the '6,' we count by fives together—"5, 10, 15…"—until we get to the '12' (thirty). Then I say,

"So, how much time longer do we have? We have 30 minutes. Now you know how to tell how much time is left on your own!"

We also talk about what time it is *now*.

"It is [5, 10, 15, 20, 25, 30]; it is 30 minutes *after* eight."

I explain that, "Only the little hand uses the numbers; the BIG hand is what we use to know how much time we have. And we count the minutes by counting by 'fives.'" I also explain that we tell the hour by looking at the number *after* where the little hand is: since the little hand is after the "8," we say "eight."

Being able to use time on their own helps children with autism self-regulate. Time is now predictable, and they can figure it out "on their own." Once they know language to read a clock, and how to use time, I may repeat this exercise other times throughout this session, and other sessions. For example, when I see the child looking at the clock because she is tired of what we're doing, I can tell her,

"We need to do this for five more minutes? Look at the clock. See when five more minutes is? That's when we're done with this."

This way, on her own, she can independently track what we're doing and how much longer until we stop.

Assisting with Arithmetic

Children with ASD often have difficulty keeping their brains focused on the relevant information in front of them. Solving even a simple arithmetic problem can be confusing; the child is reading a number, 346, but is expected to make computations based on individual numerals—3, 4, 6—and not the number. In the example below, we read or say "three hundred forty-six plus twenty-four," but computational instructions are based on the individual numerals.

$$346$$
$$+\ 24$$

> "First, you add the last number of the top number, '6,' and the last number of the bottom number, '4.' This equals ten. Place the zero under the line under the four in 24, and put a little 1 above the 4 in 346."

This can be especially confusing verbally because the teacher is referring to several numbers that are all different. The teacher is referring to two of the numbers, 6 on the top and 4 on the bottom, while implicitly referring to two other numbers, 346 on the top and 24 on the bottom, and separating the 1 in 10 from the 0 in 10. In addition, there are directional instructions—"top," "left," "bottom," "above," "below"—all referring to different numbers, with some numbers made up of other numbers—346 is different than just 6 even though 346 includes a 6; 24 includes the number 2, even though we don't call it a two, except when we're doing the computation and the teacher says, "Add the 4 in 346 and the 2 in 24."

Despite this verbal confusion, I have found that many children with ASD know *how* to do addition, and even multiplication. However, they get confused by visual presentation of so many numbers. To simplify their visual task, I teach them a variation of the "reading finger," this time applying it to arithmetic problems.

I help the child point her finger at the numbers as she verbally works through the problem, moving her finger towards each number she's saying. This allows her to slow down her brain and focus on each number one at a time. In most cases, I have found that the arithmetic problems that the child was struggling with were not because she didn't know *how* to add or multiply, but that she wasn't able to properly attend to the individual numerals (numbers) that she needed to use in the computation. By using her "math finger" she was suddenly able to correctly answer problems on her arithmetic homework that previously caused her frustration.

Part V

FINAL THOUGHTS

CHAPTER 17

Reminders When Implementing *Thinking in Speech*

DOs When Working with Children with ASD

Teach a child to verbally express his feelings.

Understanding one's emotional state requires the child to have the ability to differentially name the varying degrees of intensity he can feel in any given situation, and how to adapt or react accordingly. For example, "irritated" has a very different behavioral response than "enraged." Many stressful situations can cause the same "tightening of the gut." That tightening in the gut is a physical expression of an emotional situation. Sometimes it occurs when one is feeling unhappy, but it can also occur when one is feeling very excited. By developing inner speech the child can first categorize the feeling— good versus bad, happy versus sad, and so on—and then develop more refined labels for similar emotions: bored versus angry versus indifferent versus stressed; or happy versus fabulous versus spunky. By being able to label and speak the emotion ("I feel angry"), the child is able to communicate his feeling (anger) rather than act it out (throw something or hit someone).

Teach a child to understand when he's feeling tired and needs to stop.

When a child gets tired, he can emotionally dysregulate, which can result in his acting out. It is important for the child to understand what "tired" feels like so that he can verbally express this to the adult, thereby replacing the acting-out behavior. Pausing or resting in response to the feeling of being tired is one way to prevent emotional dysregulation from occurring. Another strategy is for the child to learn to pace himself. This occurs by helping the child to develop inner speech. The adult models the inner dialogue by stating, "Your brain is showing me tired; your brain is begging you to stop. Your brain is begging you to say, 'I'm tired, please stop.' This is what tired feels like. When I hear 'I'm tired, can we stop?' then we'll stop." The adult then waits for the child to imitate, "I'm tired, can we stop?" The adult then praises the child for helping the adult understand that he is tired.

Teach a child that learning is hard, and that what he's feeling is what we call "hard."

Getting "stuck" on a homework problem causes stress. A child with impoverished inner speech will respond to the stress by tearing up the paper, or throwing the paper away, or screaming, "I can't do this." A child with ASD needs to be explicitly taught that learning is hard, *not that he can't do it*. The "problem" is *the task*, not himself. We get to call a task "easy" after we practice it.

Teach a child how to ask for help.

We all know adults who are reluctant to ask for help; they simply don't want to. In contrast, many children with ASD don't know they *need* to. And equally importantly, they don't know how to ask for help. As with other behaviors, they will often act out the frustration they are feeling, rather than reason through how to solve the problem. Asking for help is part of problem-solving. The adult should explicitly describe the child's behavior to the child; the adult then interprets the child's behavior to the child (e.g. "When you roll your eyes and throw your book on the floor, you are showing me that you need help. When I hear 'This is hard, I need help,' I can help you. I don't understand yelling or throwing, but I do understand 'I need help.'" Then the adult quietly adds, "Let me know when you are ready," and waits for the child to express the need for help. The adult then praises the child for expressing his need for assistance, so that the adult can help him.

Teach a child how to adapt to new situations.

We learn about the world around us through personal experiences and watching/listening to others; this is called world knowledge. To successfully adapt to new situations, a child needs to activate world knowledge (e.g. every experience he has personally experienced, heard, eavesdropped on, watched), and compare and contrast the choices made during his life experiences, in order to decide on a logical response to the current situation or problem. Teaching a child how to adapt involves helping the child develop inner speech.

DON'Ts: What *Not* to Do When Working with Children with ASD

As any adult knows, whether parent, teacher or clinician, as rewarding as it is to see the developments that children with ASD make over time, working with children with ASD also has its challenging moments. As a clinician helping these children develop their problem-solving skills, I am, by definition, putting these children in situations requiring them to solve a "problem." For the child these are stressful situations. Stated another way, I am making the child feel stressed. And as noted previously, I want the child to use language to talk themselves through the stress they are feeling as well as to participate in the task, or solve the problem I have given them. This means that I have to always remind myself that *I am the cause of their stress.* Therefore, it is also my responsibility to not blame the child when they don't perform the way I want them to, or become emotionally dysregulated.

Below are my inner-speech reminders that I tell myself when I see resistance, reluctance or dysregulation in the child with whom I am working.

DON'T assume the child will be able to efficiently use his previously learned knowledge for problem-solving.

As noted previously, children with ASD have difficulty making logical, independent choices. The ability to do this requires comparing one's previously learned knowledge with a current situation or context, and then adapting one's behavior or response accordingly. Children with ASD will have difficulty with vague or abstract language

("That wasn't nice" or "pay attention" are examples of abstract language—what does "nice" mean? What does "paying attention" look like?). Equally importantly, they have insufficient self-insight to understand when they can independently finish something and when they will need to ask for help.

DON'T use negative reinforcement as a means to modify the child's behavior.

Children with ASD have a limited ability to use self-reflection and self-insight as a means for learning how to independently adapt and change their behavior or responses. What appears to be "acting out" is really the result of feeling frustrated by the task and not being able to express one's feelings about it. When we analyze what it is about the task that is causing the frustration, and what we can do to decrease the stress (e.g. provide more visual support, use simpler language), we can then help the child express their feelings, increase their coping skills and return to the learning tasks.

DON'T assume the child is not interested in learning, based on his behavior or response.

Wanting to learn is natural in children; they are naturally curious. Unfortunately, the cognitive glitches these children have make it especially hard for these children to channel their natural curiosity into functional learning and problem-solving. It is their frustration as a result of decreased understanding for problem-solving that causes them to act out, not a lack of motivation.

DON'T take the behavior or response personally.

If you've ever undergone physical therapy, you know that exercising those damaged bones, muscles and ligaments *hurts!* For children with ASD, learning is hard; exercising their brain *hurts!* Children don't have the understanding that the short-term discomfort they experience during challenging tasks will be rewarded by long-term knowledge. Children with ASD need to be explicitly taught this lesson, by repeatedly being told how smart they are, and that after they practice, it will get easier!

DON'T assume negative behavior means the child doesn't care about you!

Children are people-pleasers! Regardless of behavior or response, all children want to earn our approval and respect. Our job, whether as parents, teachers, counselors or therapists, is to empathize with their stress and frustration, and always reassure them that we will be there to help them, no matter how challenging a task we put in front of them.

THE FIVE DOS AND DON'TS WHEN TEACHING PROBLEM-SOLVING TO CHILDREN WITH ASD

DO:

- teach a child to verbally express his feelings

- teach a child when to understand when he's feeling tired and needs to stop

- teach a child that learning is hard, and that what he's feeling is what we call "hard"

- teach a child how to ask for help

- teach a child how to adapt to new situations.

DON'T:

- assume the child will be able to efficiently use his previously learned knowledge for problem-solving

- use negative reinforcement as a means to modify his behavior

- assume the child is not interested in learning, based on his behavior or response

- take the behavior or response personally

- assume negative behavior means the child doesn't care about you!

References

Abott, B. B., and Baddia, P. (1986). "Predictable versus unpredictable shock conditions and physiological measures of stress: A reply to Arthur." *Psychological Bulletin 100*, 384–387.

Akbar, M., Loomis, R., and Paul, R. (2013). "The interplay of language on executive functions in children with ASD." *Research in Autism Spectrum Disorders 7*, 494–501.

Alderson-Day, B., and Fernyhough, C. (2015). "Inner speech: Development, cognitive functions, phenomenology, and neurobiology." *Psychological Bulletin 141*, 931–965.

American Psychiatric Association (2000). *Diagnostic and Statistical Manual of Mental Disorders, Fourth Edition (DSM-IV-TR)*. Washington, DC: American Psychiatric Association.

American Psychiatric Association (2013). *Diagnostic and Statistical Manual of Mental Disorders, Fifth Edition (DSM-5)*. Arlington, VA: American Psychiatric Publishing.

Aro, T., Laakso, M., Määttä, S., Tolvanen, A., and Poikkeus, M. (2014). "Associations between toddler-age communication and kindergarten-age self-regulatory skills." *Journal of Speech, Language, and Hearing Research 57*, 1405–1417.

Baddeley, A. D. (2003). "Working memory: Looking back and looking forward." *Nature Reviews 4*, 10, 829–839.

Baldo, J. V., Dronkers, N. F., Wilkins, D., Ludy, C., Raskin, P., and Kim, J. Y. (2005). "Is problem solving dependent on language?" *Brain and Language 92*, 240–250.

Banich, M. T. (2004). *Cognitive Neuroscience and Neuropsychology*. Boston, MA: Hough Mifflin.

Barkley, R. A. (1997). "Behavioral inhibition, sustained attention, and executive functions: Constructing a unifying theory of ADHD." *Psychological Bulletin 121*, 65–94.

Barneveld, P. S., Swaab, H., van Engeland, H., and de Sonnevill, L. (2014). "Cross-sectional evidence for a decrease in cognitive function with age in children with autism spectrum disorders?" *Autism Research 7*, 527–534.

Baron-Cohen, S. (2000). "Theory of Mind and Autism: A Fifteen Year Review." In S. Baron-Cohen, H. Tager-Flusberg and D. J. Cohen (eds.) *Understanding Other Minds: Perspectives from Developmental Cognitive Neuroscience,* second edition. New York, NY: Oxford University Press.

Baron-Cohen, S., Golan, O., and Ashwin, E. (2009). "Can emotion recognition be taught to children with autism spectrum conditions?" *Philosophical Transactions of the Royal Society B 364,* 1567–3574.

Baron-Cohen, S., Leslie, A. M., and Frith, U. (1985) "Does the autistic child have a 'theory of mind'?" *Cognition 21,* 1, 37–46.

Barrett, L. R., Tugade, M. M., and Engle, R. W. (2004). "Individual differences in working memory capacity and dual-process theories of mind." *Psychological Bulletin 130,* 553–573.

Basar, K., Sesia, T., Groenewegen, H., Steinbusch, H. W., Visser-Vandewall, V., and Temel, Y. (2010). "Nucleus accumbens and impulsivity." *Progress in Neurobiology 92,* 533–557.

Behan, B., Stone, A., and Garavan, H. (2015). "Right prefrontal and striatum interactions underlying impulsive choice and impulsive responding." *Human Brain Mapping 36,* 187–195.

Belmonte, M. K., Cook, E. H., Jr., Anderson, G. M., Rubenstein, J. L., et al. (2004). "Autism as a disorder of neural information processing: Directions for research and targets for therapy." *Molecular Psychiatry 9,* 646–663.

Bialystock, E., Sherry, S. B., Shanker, S., and Codd, J. (2003). "Executive function deficits in children with autism." *Interdisciplinary Council on Developmental and Learning Disorders 7,* 37–55.

Boucugnani, L. L., and Jones, R. W. (1989). "Behaviors analogous to frontal lobe dysfunction in children with attention deficit hyperactivity disorder." *Archives of Clinical Neuropsychology 4,* 161–173.

Brandimonte, M. A., Filippello, P., Coluccia, E., Altgassen, M., and Kliegel, M. (2011). "To do or not to do? Prospective memory versus response inhibition in autism spectrum disorder and attention-deficit/hyperactivity disorder." *Memory 19,* 1, 56–66.

Burack, J. A., Russo, N., Dawkins, T., and Huizinga, M. (2010). "Developments and Regressions in Rule Use: The Case of Zinedine Zidane." In B. W. Sokol, J. Carpendale, U. Müller, A. Young and G. Iarocci (eds.) *Self- and Social-Regulation: Exploring the Relations Between Social Interaction, Social Understanding, and the Development of Executive Functions.* Oxford: Oxford University Press.

Burgess, G. C., Gray, J. R., Conway, A. R. A., and Braver, T. S. (2011). "Neural mechanisms of interference control underlie the relationship between fluid intelligence and working memory span." *Journal of Experimental Psychology: General 140,* 674–692.

Capps, L., Yirmiya, N., and Sigman, M. (1992). "Understanding of simple and complex emotions in non-retarded children with autism." *Journal of Child Psychology and Psychiatry 33,* 1169–1182.

Channon, S. (2004). "Frontal lobe dysfunction and everyday problem-solving: Social and non-social contributions." *Acta Psychologica 115*, 235–254.

Channon, S., and Crawford, S. (1999) "Problem-solving in real-life-type situations: The effects of anterior and posterior lesions on performance." *Neuropsychologia 37*, 757–770.

Chiu, P. H., Kayali, M. A., Kishida, K.T, Tomlin, D., et al. (2008). "Self responses along cingulate cortex reveal quantitative neural phenotype for high-functioning autism." *Neuron 57*, 463–473.

Chuderski, A., and Nęcka, E. (2012). "The contribution of working memory to fluid reasoning: Capacity, control, or both?" *Journal of Experimental Psychology: Learning, Memory, and Cognition 38*, 6, 1689–1710.

Dalley, J. W., Fryer, T. D., Brichard, L., Robinson, E. S. J., et al. (2007). "Nucleus accumbens D2/3 receptors predict trait impulsivity and cocaine reinforcement." *Science 315*, 1267–1270.

Damasio, A.R., Everitt, B.J., and Bishop, D. (1996). "The somatic marker hypothesis and the possible functions of the prefrontal cortex [and discussion]." *Philosophical Transactions of the Royal Society B 351*, 1413–1420.

Dapretto, M., Davies, M. S., Pfeifer, J. H., Scott, A. A., et al. (2006). "Understanding emotions in others: Mirror neuron dysfunction in children with autism spectrum disorders." *Nature Neuroscience 9*, 28–30.

Diamond, A., and Lee, K. (2011). "Interventions shown to aid executive function development in children 4 to 12 years old." *Science 333*, 959–964.

Dinstein, I., Heeger, D.J., Lorenzi, L., Minshew, N.J., Malach, R., and Behrmann, M. (2012). "Unreliable evoked responses in autism." *Neuron 75*, 981–991.

Dunbar, K., and Sussman, D. (1995). "Toward a cognitive account of frontal lobe function: Simulating frontal lobe deficits in normal subjects." *Structure and Functions of the Human Prefrontal Cortex 769*, 289–304.

D'Zurilla, T. J. and Maydeu-Olivares, A. (1995). "Conceptual and methodological issues in social problem-solving assessment." *Behavior Therapy 26*, 3, 409–432.

Elliott, R. (2003). "Executive functions and their disorders: Imaging in clinical neuroscience." *British Medical Bulletin 65*, 1, 49–59.

Fahy, J. K. (2014). "Language and executive functions: Self-talk for self-regulation." *SIG 1 Perspectives on Language Learning and Education 21*, 61–71.

Fernyhough, C. (1996). "The dialogic mind: A dialogic approach to the higher mental functions." *New Ideas in Psychology 14*, 47–62.

Fernyhough, C. (2004). "Alien voices and inner dialogue: Towards a developmental account of auditory verbal hallucinations." *New Ideas in Psychology 22*, 49–68.

Fernyhough, C. (2008). "Getting Vygotskian about theory of mind: Mediation, dialogue, and the development of social understanding." *Developmental Review 28*, 225–262.

Fernyhough, C. (2009). "Dialogic Thinking." In A. Winsler, C. Fernyhough and I. Montero (eds.) *Private Speech, Executive Functioning, and the Development of Verbal Self-Regulation*. Cambridge: Cambridge University Press.

Fernyhough, C. (2010). "Vygotsky, Luria, and the Social Brain." In B. W. Sokol, U. Müller, J. I. M. Carpendale, A. R. Young and G. Iarocci (eds.), *Self and Socialization: Social Interaction and the Development of Social Understanding and Executive Functions.* Oxford: Oxford University Press.

Galotti, K. M. (1989). "Approaches to studying formal and everyday reasoning." *Psychological Bulletin 105,* 331–351.

Gillespie-Lynch, K., Sepeta, L., Wang, Y., Marshall, S., et al. (2012). "Early childhood predictors of the social competence of adults with autism." *Journal of Autism and Developmental Disorders 42,* 161–174.

Gershkoff-Stowe, L., and Hahn, H. R. (2007). "Fast mapping skills in the developing lexicon." *Journal of Speech, Language, and Hearing Research 50,* 682–697.

Goldstein, F. C., and Levin, H. S. (1987). "Disorders of Reasoning and Problem-Solving Ability." In M. J. Meier, A. L. Benton and L. Diller (eds.) *Neuropsychological Rehabilitation.* New York: Guilford Press.

Grandin, T. (1995). "How People with Autism Think." In E. Schoer and G. B. Mesilbov (eds.) *Learning and Cognition in Autism.* New York: Pleneum Press.

Grandin, T. (1996). *Thinking in Pictures: Other Reports from My Life with Autism.* New York: Vintage Books.

Gray, K. M., and Tonga, B. J. (2005). "Screening for autism in infants and preschool children with developmental delay." *Australian and New Zealand Journal of Psychiatry 39,* 378–386.

Gross, J. J. (1998). "The emerging field of emotion regulation: An integrative review." *Review of General Psychology 2,* 271–299.

Gross, J. J. (2014). "Emotion Regulation: Conceptual and Empirical Foundations." In J. J. Gross (ed.) *Handbook of Emotion Regulation, second edition.* New York: Guilford Press.

Gross, J. J., and Thompson, R. A. (2007). "Emotion Regulation: Conceptual Foundations." In J. J. Gross (ed.) *Handbook of Emotion Regulation, second edition.* New York: Guilford Press.

Gruber, O., and Goschke, T. (2004). "Executive control emerging from dynamic interactions between brain systems mediating language, working memory and attentional processes." *Acta Psychologica 115,* 105–121.

Harris, P. L., de Rosnay, M., and Pons, F. (2005). "Language and children's understanding of mental states." *Current Directions in Psychological Science 14,* 69–73.

Herry, C., Bach, D. R., Esposito, F., Di Salle, F., et al. (2007). "Processing of temporal unpredictability in human and animal amygdala." *Journal of Neuroscience 27,* 5958–5966.

Hill, E. L. (2004). "Executive dysfunction in autism." *Trends in Cognitive Science 8,* 1, 26–32.

Hoskyn, M. (2010). "Working Memory in Infancy and Early Childhood: What Develops?" In B. W. Sokol, U. Müller, J. I. M. Carpendale, A. R. Young and G. Iarocci (eds.) *Self and Socialization: Social Interaction and the Development of Social Understanding and Executive Functions.* Oxford: Oxford University Press.

Hrabok, M., and Kerns, K. A. (2010). "The Development of Self-regulation: A Neuropsychological Perspective." In B. W. Sokol, U. Müller, J. I. M. Carpendale, A. R. Young and G. Iarocci (eds.) *Self and Socialization: Social Interaction and the Development of Social Understanding and Executive Functions.* Oxford: Oxford University Press.

Humphreys, K., Hasson, U., Avidan, G., Minshew, N. J., and Behrmann, M. (2008). "Cortical patterns of category-selective activation for faces, places and objects in adults with autism." *Autism Research 1*, 52–63.

Just, M. A, Cherkassky, V. L., Keller, T. A., Kana, R. K., and Minshew, N. J. (2007). "Functional and anatomical cortical underconnectivity in autism: Evidence from an fMRI study of an executive function task and corpus callosum." *Cerebral Cortex 17*, 951–961.

Just, M. A. and Keller, T. A. (2013). "Is 'underconnectivity' in autism specific to frontal cortex?" *Spectrum*, March 22. Available at https://spectrumnews. org/opinion/viewpoint/is-underconnectivity-in-autism-specific-to-frontal-cortex (accessed December 4, 2017).

Just, M. A., Keller, T. A., Malave, K. L., Kana, R. K., and Varma, S. (2013). "Autism as a neural systems disorder: A theory of frontal–posterior underconnectivity." *Neuroscience and Biobehavioral Reviews 36*, 4, 1292–1313.

Klinger, L. G., Klinger, M. R., and Pohlig, R. L. (2006). "Implicit learning impairments in autism spectrum disorders." In J. M. Perez, P. M. González, M. L. Comi and C. Nieto (eds.) *New Developments in Autism. The Future Is Today.* London: Jessica Kingsley Publishers.

Lakin, J. L., and Chartrand, T. L. (2003). "Using nonconscious behavioral mimicry to create affiliation and rapport." *Psychological Science: A Journal of the American Psychological Society 14*, 334–339.

Landry, S. H., Miller-Loncar, C. L., Smith, K. E., and Swank, P. R. (2002). "The role of parenting in children's development of executive processes." *Developmental Neuropsychology 21*, 15–41.

Lezak, M. D. (1995). *Neuropsychological Assessment.* New York : Oxford University Press.

Luria, A. R. (1966). *Human Brain and Psychological Processes.* New York: Harper and Row.

Malloy, P. F., Cohen, R. A., and Jenkins, M. A. (1998). "Frontal Lobe Function and Dysfunction." In P. J. Snyder and P. D. Nussbaum (eds.) *Clinical Neuropsychology: A Pocket Handbook for Assessment.* Washington, DC: American Psychological Association.

McCabe, D. P., Roediger, H. L, McDaniel, M. A., Balota, D. A., and Hambrick, D. Z. (2010). "The relationship between working memory capacity and executive functioning: Evidence for a common executive attention construct." *Neuropsychology 24*, 222–243.

McClure, S. M., Laibson, D. I., Loewenstein, G., and Cohen, J. D. (2004). "Separate neural systems value immediate and delayed monetary rewards." *Science 306*, 503–507.

McDonald, S. (2007). "The social, emotional and cultural life of the orbitofrontal cortex." *Brain Impairment 8*, 41–51.

McGregor, K. K., and Bean, A. (2012). "How children with autism extend new words." *Journal of Speech, Language, and Hearing Research 55*, 70–83.

Metcalfe, J., and Mischel, W. (1999). "A hot/cool system analysis of delay of gratification: Dynamics of willpower." *Psychological Review 106*, 3–19.

Miller, C. A. (2006). "Developmental relationships between language and Theory of Mind." *American Journal of Speech-Language Pathology 15*, 142–154.

Minshew, N. J., Goldstein, G., and Siegel, D. J. (1997). "Neuropsychologic functioning in autism: Profile of a complex information processing disorder." *Journal of the International Neuropsychological Society 3*, 303–316.

Miyake, A., Emerson, M. J., Padilla, F., and Ahn, J. (2004). "Inner speech as a retrieval aid for task goals: The effects of cue type and articulatory suppression in the random task cuing paradigm." *Acta Psychologica 115*, 123–142.

Nathan, J. (2011). "Growing up in a family with autism." *The All Aboard News: A Quarterly Publication from the Advisory Board on Autism and Related Disorders 4*, 1. Available at http://autism-support.org/wp-content/uploads/2011/05/ABOARD_Newsletter_Winter_2010.pdf (accessed December 3, 2017).

Ochsner, K. N., and Gross, J. J. (2005). "The cognitive control of emotion." *Trends in Cognitive Science 9*, 242–249.

O'Hearn, K., Asato, M., Ordaz, S., and Luna, B. (2008). "Neurodevelopment and executive function in autism." *Developmental Psychopathology 20*, 1103–1132.

Pellicano, E. (2007). "Links between theory of mind and executive function in young children with autism: Clues to development primacy." *Developmental Psychology 43*, 974–990.

Pelphrey, K. A., Morris, J. P., and McCarthy, G. (2005). "Neural basis of eye gaze processing deficits in autism." *Brain 128*, 1038–1048.

Pennington, B. F., and Ozonoff, S. (1996). "Executive functions and developmental psychopathology." *Journal of Child Psychology and Psychiatry 37*, 51–87.

Perry, R. J., and Hodges, J. R. (1999). "Attention and executive deficits in Alzheimer's disease. A critical review." *Brain 122*, 3, 383–404.

Piaget, J. (1923/1959). *The Language and Thought of the Child.* New York: Meridian Books.

Pliszka, S. R. (2003). *Neuroscience for the Mental Health Clinician.* New York: Gilford Press.

Rajmohan, V. and Mohandas, E. (2007). "Mirror neuron system." *Indian Journal of Psychiatry 49*, 1, 66–69.

Rath, J. F., Hennessy, J. J., and Diller, L. (2003). "Social problem solving and community integration in postacute rehabilitation outpatients with traumatic brain injury." *Rehabilitation Psychology 48*, 3, 137–144.

Reber, A. S. (1989). "Implicit learning and tacit knowledge." *Journal of Experimental Psychology: General 118*, 219–235.

Redcay, E., and Courchesne, E. (2008). "Deviant functional magnetic resonance imaging patterns of brain activity to speech in 2–3-year-old children with autism spectrum disorder." *Biological Psychiatry 64*, 2008, 589–598.

Richard, G. J., and Fahy, J. K. (2005). *The Source for Development of Executive Functions.* East Moline, IL: LinguiSystems, Inc.

Richland, L. E., and Burchina, M. R. (2013). "Early executive function predicts reasoning development." *Psychological Science 24,* 87–92.

Royall, D. R., Cordes, J. A., and Polk, M. (1998). "CLOX: An Executive Clock Drawing Task." *Journal of Neurology, Neurosurgery, and Psychiatry 64,* 588–594.

Salthouse, T. A. (2005). "Relations between cognitive abilities and measures of executive functioning." *Neuropsychology 19,* 4, 532–545.

Sandson, J., and Albert, M. L. (1984). "Varieties of perseveration." *Neuropsychologia 22,* 715–732.

Shaheen, S. (2014). "How child's play impacts executive function-related behaviors." *Applied Neuropsychology: Child 3,* 182–187.

Silliman, E. R., and Berninger, V. W. (2011). "Cross-disciplinary dialogue about the nature of oral and written language problems in the context of developmental, academic, and phenotypic profile." *Topics in Language Disorders 31,* 1, 6–23.

Singer, B. D., and Bashir, A. S. (1999). "What are executive functions and self-regulation and what do they have to do with language-learning disorders?" *Speech, Language, and Hearing Services in Schools 30,* 3, 265–273.

Sinha, P., Kjelgaard, M. M., Gandhi, T. K., Tsourides, K., Cardinaux, A. L., Pantazis, D., et al. (2014). "Autism as a disorder of prediction." *Proceedings of the National Academy of Sciences 111,* 15220–15225.

Sohlberg, M. M., and Mateer, C. A. (2001). *Cognitive Rehabilitation: An Integrative Neuropsychological Approach.* Andover: Taylor and Francis Books Ltd.

Sparks, Sarah D. (2012). "Scientists find learning is not 'hard-wired'." *Education Week,* June 4. Available at www.edweek.org/ew/articles/2012/06/06/33neuroscience_ep.h31.html (accessed December 3, 2017).

Spunt, R. P. (2013). "Mirroring, mentalizing, and the social neuroscience of listening." *International Journal of Listening 27,* 61–72.

Stuss, D. T., and Anderson, V. (2004). "The frontal lobes and theory of mind: Developmental concept from adult focal lesion research." *Brain and Cognition 55,* 69–83.

Stuss, D. T., Gallup, G. G., and Alexander, M. P. (2001). "The frontal lobes are necessary for 'theory of mind.'" *Brain 124,* 279–286.

Tranel, D., Anderson, S. W., and Benton, A. (1994). "Development of the Concept of 'Executive Function' and Its Relationship to the Frontal Lobes." In F. Boller and J. Grafman (eds.) *Handbook of Neuropsychology* (Vol. 8). Amsterdam: Elsevier.

Troyer, A. K., Graves, R. E., and Cullum, K. M. (1994). "Executive functioning as a mediator of the relationship between age and episodic memory in healthy aging." *Aging and Cognition 1,* 45–53.

Tuokko, H., and Hadjistavropoulos, T. (1998). *An Assessment Guide To Geriatric Neuropsychology.* Mahwah, NJ: Erlbaum.

Vosniadou, S., and Brewer, W. F. (1987). "Theories of knowledge restructuring in development." *Review of Educational Research 57*, 51–67.

Vygotsky, L. S. (1986). *Thought and Language*, edited by A. Kozulin. Cambridge, MA: The MIT Press.

Vygotsky, L. S. (1987 [1934]). "Thinking and speech." In *The Collected Works of L. S. Vygotsky* (Vol. 1). New York: Plenum.

Ward, S., and Jacobsen, K. (2014). "Executive function situational awareness observation tool." *SIG 16 Perspectives on School-Based Issues 15*, 164–173.

Weiss, J. A., Thomson, K., and Chan, L. (2014). "A systematic literature review of emotion regulation measurement in individuals with autism spectrum disorder." *Autism Research 7*, 629–648.

Whitehouse, A. J. O., Mayberry, M. T., and Durkin, K. (2006). "Inner speech impairments in autism." *Journal of Child Psychology and Psychiatry 47*, 857–865.

Williams, D. M., Bowler, D. M., and Jarrold, C. (2012). "Inner speech is used to mediate short-term memory, but not planning, among intellectually high-functioning adults with autism spectrum disorder." *Development and Psychopathology 24*, 225–239.

Woodcock, R. W., and Johnson, M. D. (1990). *Woodcock–Johnson Psycho-Educational Battery—Revised*. Allen, TX: DLM Teaching Resources.

Zelazo, P. D., and Müller, U. (2002). "Executive Function in Typical and Atypical Development." In U. Goswami (ed.) *Blackwell Handbook of Childhood Cognitive Development*. Malden, MA: Blackwell Publishers.

Zenko, C. (2014). "Practical solutions for executive function challenges created by the unique learning styles of students with autism spectrum disorder (ASD)." *SIG 16 Perspectives on School-Based Issues 15*, 141–150.

Subject Index

Author Index